GOOD HEALTH
IS THE
NEW WEALTH!

by
LADY WISE

GOOD HEALTH
IS THE
NEW WEALTH!

by
LADY WISE

Letter of Introduction

Aloha Mahalo!

Thanks in advance for choosing to read my latest book and taking a step closer to empowering yourself with good health, vitality and an abundance of joy and wealth in your sacred life!

Aloha is an invocation of that beautiful divine spark that resides within each one of us and is filled with love, compassion, kindness, grace and affection. Mahalo is a divine blessing of gratitude and thanks.

I am so thankful that you have made a choice point to take better care of YOU! At any time, and particularly at this challenging mark in history as we are facing the impact from COVID-19 (the very first coronavirus outbreak formally recognised by the World Health Organisation as a pandemic), priority of our health and happiness must surely come top of our list? There is no chance that you are reading this book! Indeed, there is a purpose for everything that happens. You are alive at a very auspicious time and everything that you have experienced up until now has meaning.

There is no coincidence that another word for 'corona' is crown. The Crown Chakra is one of the chakras in the chakra system about which I will be explaining more and I devote a whole chapter to how it fits in to our remarkable system of consciousness. The birthright of this specific chakra is 'to know' and it governs awareness, understanding and self-knowledge. Isn't that interesting? Indeed, metaphorically speaking, it is the equivalent of our body's operating system as it is connected to the unified field of energy throughout the universe. It is in this energy of consciousness, of all that is, where, as a multi-dimensional human being (which all of us are whether you believe it or not), we have unlimited access to the universe in all its majesty and miracles. The strength of this connection determines our level of consciousness. The higher the level at which we operate, the greater the joy, good health, longevity of life and abundance that we will experience.

This morning I awakened at 4.01am and put on some of my favourite Solfeggio music as a beautifully calming influence wafting throughout my home. I had fully intended going back to sleep but as often happens, a fleeting intuitive thought 'popped' into my head and yes, you guessed it, it was the idea to write a short book about active health and wealth. Such intuitive experiences are becoming more frequent now as I consciously work to create more ideas in a raised vibrational energy and higher frequency than before. What is even more fascinating is that when I make every attempt to ignore the intuitive thought, it persists! Do you remember that well-known phrase, 'What resists persists'? Ha! Well this idea was most definitely persisting and lying in bed was simply no longer an option. With fragranced candles lit, a cup of water and my faithful sheepskin jacket hugging my sleep rejuvenated body, I sat down at my dining room table and allowed the power of words to flow.

The content of this book on good health may, at the very least surprise you and at the very best, resonate with you as I present you with some new information that is currently only known about by approximately 2% of this planet. Remember that we do not know what we do not know. It will rely on your 'knowingness' and resonation with core truth about what I write. The multi-verse has a remarkable way of working with the potentials and dreams of human beings to guide them to what they need when they need it. It is an amazing support network about which we are only just beginning to understand. We are alive on earth at this time as part of an elegant system of compassion that is evolving for humanity. It has been known about by the indigenous for thousands of years and is celebrated outside of linearity.

"

It is about individual consciousness of compassion
and care for other human beings.
~ Kryon

This paradigm of compassion and caring is the essence of peace on earth and comes with the maturity of human beings who have started to work the puzzle of life. Good health is one of the key outcomes at the core of this understanding, for without it we cannot function effectively and feel the joy and aliveness of life every day which is our birthright.

Moreover, it is only when we are operating with a healthy, functioning body that we are we in the best position to help and support others with our strength, love, compassion, grace and wisdom.

When we are faced with a challenge of any kind, it is all too easy for us to feel unworthy and question whether we even have a right to exist in this society. Let me assure you that you do have a right to exist in this amazing world and that you are so unique and magnificent and yet you do not always know it. We are born with some weaknesses in order that we can grow and evolve these into our strengths. Look at how Ghandi and Martin Luther King were each able in their own way to turn around their initial apparent lack of being heard by others into successful leadership!

I love the fact that through social media every person has a greater opportunity than ever before to have their voice heard. It is so rewarding and such a privilege to be able to have the platform to enthuse and help others grow in their wisdom, especially when this potential leads others to become more informed about who they are and to have good health!

"

We are each so unique with the talents we bring
An aptitude to write, perhaps paint and/or sing?
Whatever your gifts, feel alive doing your thing
For such creativity is truly inspiring!
~ Lady Wise

There is no need to worry or become anxious when you cannot think of what you love to do or know what your gifts are, for example. Many of us have so many hidden talents that we have yet to discover and have no idea about the potentials of ourselves!

I never knew I would start writing and indeed start writing so much until I experienced the passing of my best friend who was my Mum. In my naïvity I thought I would write

a 'Tips Guide' to help those individuals visiting their loved-ones and friends in hospital based on my own personal experience with her. It was only several years later when I was persistently asked the question of why I had written my first book, that I had an eureka moment in realising that this had been my own way of dealing with my grief. This was my way of channelling this negative energy into a positive purpose with the aim of helping others going through a similar challenge. I slowly regained my own personal power which made me feel worthy of continuing to live and to choose to live in love. I found a way to step into the individuality of who I am as a happy, joy-filled, loving person of humanity, able to appreciate all that is in both its invisible and visible forms within the electromagnetic spectrum of the rich and diverse galaxy.

Why would you deny yourself the best life that you could ever have, when you are responsible for creating it? Every detail experienced in your life is for you to acknowledge and remember. Expect good things and they will happen!

"

Since 2012 a new era has begun
It is up to the Self to create good fun
Love and laughter bring good health,
Balance, harmony and an abundance of wealth.
~ Lady Wise

For too long now, many of us have been rushing around making excuses to do everything for our family and perhaps even friends without taking time to stop and to make the time to do something for ourselves. There will never be another time in the evolution of humanity than the fast-track

opportunity that is being given to us right now to relax and to carefully rethink and reassess our whole life. It is time to reconsider the importance of every relationship that you have and to use this unique window of possibilities to determine what exactly you are doing and what you want to do with your precious, sacred life. It is that simple.

The new adventure awaiting you beckons you to question,'Is there really more to me than the physical body I see when I look in the mirror?' Have you ever thought that perhaps there is something bigger in the universe of which you are a part? Perhaps you might ask yourself, 'Is there knowledge and understanding within me (of which I am capable of unleashing) that would transform my current thinking and set me on a trajectory of love and integrity, truth and kindness, benevolence and compassion?'

The answer, my friend, is and always will be, 'Yes...if you want it!' This is the gift that is in this book for you when you decide on your own to take a step, metaphorically, into the unknown in complete trust that there is indeed so much more in the multi-verse which waits patiently to connect with you, to support you in all you do and to love you beyond all measure as you grow into the beautiful, sacred, loving human being that is the essence of who you truly are.

No-one can take you on this soulful journey of adventure. Only you have the power within of consciousness that awakens to ask for more information about who you are at a soul level. This may be the only journey that you want to take on your own when you first 'open the door', take a deep breath and realise that the richness of life is invested within your soul.

Your soul does not recognise the external, visible wealth obtained from material assets. I can assure you that this book will guide you to question the value of everything that you do and to enjoy discovering more about the best version of yourself. This is beautiful! This is who you are! Oh yes, and did I happen to mention that there is a few side effects to this challenge of the unknown adventure of self-truth and rainbow light? It will lead you to have good health, joy and abundance in your life of love! One of my own favourite sayings is:-

"

Truly in this process you become a Master of yourself
Without reliance on others, you can create your own
good health and wealth
Embrace playfulness with open arms
And allow this to become one of your charms!

I am sending you positive vibes of good health and wealth as you say, 'Hello to love!' and your own spirit of adventure. Remember that life and the universe know your name and love YOU unconditionally!

Mahalo kokua!

With love and gratitude,

Lady Wise ♡
@LadyWiseWorld
www.ladywiseworld.com

Introduction

Lady Wise understands the significance of the relationship between loving what you do in all things and the choice of doing work about which you are passionate, in order to find your own inner happiness, inner contentment and success. In recent years, she has realised that only by undertaking a transformation of oneself and becoming a balanced person living in good health, harmony and working with a natural energy that is within each of us, can we find our true life purpose and fulfil our potential. This mindset can then be used in all things, personal and business to accelerate our own well-being and performance for ultimate satisfaction.

She is keen to inspire you to connect with the love that is inside of you to become a happier, balanced and healthier person living in harmony and love wherever you are and actively busy in whatever you choose to do. She knows that each of us must 'self- motivate' to be in good health and to become empowered. We must each create with total clarity of mind what it is that we desire, coupled with a sense of deserving, love and graciousness if we each want to have our own vision for the future manifested.

Lady Wise has written this book for a target audience of individuals who are keen to awaken to the truth and ability of who they are and in acknowledgement of this mastery, use that 'love power' to change the world one person at a time, starting with oneself.

It is about reconnecting with joy, good health, happiness, love and laughter and redefining our responsibility for who we are. Living a healthy life motivated by love as a driving force for good and kindness is not only immeasurably fulfilling but it may extend your own life on this planet. When a person lives their life in joy and love they are less prone to disease (dis-ease) and make no space for fear and worry. They make a conscious choice to close the door on stress and open the door to happiness! Can you imagine how much happier, healthier and more productive we would be when we can live our daily lives in balance and harmony?

Moreover, can you imagine the extra time you would have to indulge in happiness and laughter with your family and friends instead of visiting doctors' surgeries and hospitals? Indirectly this would ease the burden on our healthcare systems too!

It requires a relaxing of the linear (thinking) approach to which we have all been traditionally taught and increasingly relies on us becoming more conceptual (feeling) in how we approach solutions to our problems. What does this mean? It means that instead of thinking in a linear way, we start to feel in a conceptual way with the love that is in our heart. We have allowed ourselves over the generations to close off our emotions as human beings and thereby deprive ourselves of the greatest joy on planet earth that one can imagine – the joy of feeling, expressing and giving love!

Enjoy, embrace the truth and be exuberant in creating your own good health, abundance and happiness through the joy and power of love! Remember that everything happens for you and there is a reason for everything for your highest good! Any fear, resentment, anger and worry simply covers up the hurt within you and prevents the healing that is needed to open you up to receiving the love that you deserve. All you need to do is let love in!

Acknowledgements

Special thanks to Lee Carroll and the support entity Kryon helping in the evolution of humanity at this time, for giving me permission to share some of their knowledge and wisdom with you as I have come to understand it. Further information on Kryon's teachings may be found at www.kryon.com.

Dedication

This book is dedicated to the essence
of
Giovanna Porcaro
with whom I enjoyed
fun times and a friendship
that endures across the ripples of time!

Table of Contents

CHAPTER 1

Time to Ponder!

"

A little down-time is good for the soul
It allows you some freedom from daily patterns of control
Time to ponder on your own life as the prize
Giving you a unique opportunity to energise!
~ Lady Wise

Many of us are thinking that these are crazy times in which we presently live. And therein is the issue. Ha, ha! You are thinking! It is time to dust away the clouds of your logical mind and open up your heart to the sunshine and love that lies within! The sun has always been there for you but when you practice all your daily living from your mind then the radiant sunshine of light that exists in everyone of us never has a chance to show its glory and brilliance.

How do you really feel as you are reading this? Do you feel uncomfortable that I have suggested there is a different way to live...for example, from your heart rather than depending on your logical mind? Are you feeling annoyed with yourself because you are suddenly realising that perhaps you have been missing out on knowing and understanding a core truth all your life until now? Perhaps you are feeling thankful that someone else believes in living their life with a strong connection to their heart and you have experienced an eureka moment when all of life comes together in an 'Aha! Expression' and you know you are finally on the right path for you in the journey of soul discovery? For whatever moment it is that you are experiencing, congratulate yourself that you have made this profound connection through the power of words. This is likely to become a transformational beginning for you that will positively shape the rest of your lives! Yes, that's right, the rest of your lives – your present life, your past lives and all of your future lives as well. Is this too deep for you? I feel it is rather cool! Ha!

On a daily basis, there are more and more souls awakening to the majesty of who they are and to their inner wisdom that has been accumulated over lifetimes. I am writing principally for the benefit of the 'old souls' who are not deemed old by virtue of any linear age but who are defined by having lived at least one hundred lifetimes on planet earth already and indeed who may easily have lived more than one thousand! I am directing these words to YOU!

Until recently on planet earth only about two percent of the global population had awakened to the truth of their existence. Thankfully, due to the auspicious time in which we are choosing to live, hundreds of thousands more are now starting to awaken. This period in time is referred to as the Shift. The Pleiadians also refer to the period 2013 – 2027 as The Changeover Years.

Scientifically, planet earth is making her way through the Precession of the Equinoxes which occurs every 26,000 years. More than a 'wobble' of the earth, however, it takes a 36 year cycle (with the mid-point at 21 December 2012) for planet earth to move through the Milky Way. This mid-point 'marker' of 21 December 2012 denoted the Shift of this planet from the Barbaric Years (pre 21.12.2012) into brand new territory of a New Earth, when it achieved graduate status at this time in the galaxy for the evolution of human consciousness.

Simultaneously, it denoted the end of the Mayan calendar. This marker has been known about by all the indigenous peoples for thousands of years. The Shift is closure of the Age of Pisces which has been all about illusion, delusion and a lack of integrity. Now we are moving into the Age of Aquarius with the focus on love, truth, integrity and compassionate action as the foundation for future abundance of all kinds (including good health, relationships, families, money, economies, career and business).

Since the mid-marker point in 2012 with the scientifically proven Precession of the Equinoxes event, planet earth is living in a new paradigm never before travelled or explored. You want adventure? This lifetime is the lifetime in which to be alive because as we live throughout this Shift period, it is a one time fast-track opportunity as a human being to mature in wisdom and soul growth for one's own highest good.

"

What do you think to expanding your mind?
Would you like to know more about what goes on
deep inside?

There is a grandness and beauty beyond anything that you have ever previously been told for you to experience when you choose to know more about the magnificent human being that you are. In the marvellous words of Rumi:-

"

Yesterday I was clever, I was changing the world.
Today I am wise, I am changing myself.

To recap, all the ancestors and the indigenous peoples knew of this time and of the 21 December 2012 marker, should humanity make it...and we did! This Shift of humanity is about an evolving consciousness of all that is, a maturing of knowledge by each individual of their understanding of the soul. It is essentially a way of higher thinking.

We are living in surreal times when many communities are collapsing and there are concerns about health and the economic welfare of countries. On a positive note, these situations encourage individuals to start searching and to look at different ways to better understand themselves, to

look at new ways of doing things, to innovate, create and in doing this they find new solutions to issues and then take these out to their communities in ways that enhance the well-being of themselves and those around them.

All of these efforts are helping to bring in a new reality that is full of increased joy, abundance and good health. In order to change our habit patterns, however, we have to look closely at ourselves and recognise 'the old' in ourselves. Let me reiterate that this is nothing to do with linear age. It is to do with choosing to think, act and do things differently than we ever have before. When we choose to become more aware about who we are there is a recognition of our own old patterns or programs and old ways of doing things. When we can accept these old ways of doing things that are no longer serving us, we can allow new feelings, experiences and knowledge to come into our lives.

We are riding the edge of a new wave...of CHANGE! This, however, becomes an individual change at an energetic and cellular level first. Every thought, word and action is energy! Each feeling and thought impacts on our own energy at energetic, mental, spiritual, emotional and physical levels. When we think and feel only high thoughts without judgement then we raise our vibrational frequency and this in turn allows us to expand our mind, expand our consciousness and start to receive new higher energies and wisdom on our soul's path of growth and maturity as a human being. Indeed, in these higher energies disease or dis-ease cannot exist.

How can I simplify this? It is similar to cleaning a room. When we clear a room of clutter and tidy it up there is more space to allow for enjoyment of that room. Sometimes nothing more is needed. Less is often more when it comes to décor, character and ambience! After having tidied up the room you may now be better able to view your favourite cushions or picture on a wall. The room may even feel bigger than before and fresher too, encouraging you to spend more time in it. If it is the sitting room or living room, perhaps you may decide to move around some furniture. How many of us buy a sofa and then never move it around in the room again ever until it is time to repurpose it, refurbish it or replace it?

In a few instances, you may feel that the space you have just created from clearing away all your clutter makes way for a new favourite piece of furniture that you may have been looking at for several months on line or on display in a shop window. All of a sudden you can see where it would be ideally placed in the room for you to enjoy and appreciate! You are able to think clearly and see the potentials of the room from a different perspective once it has been tidied up.

This analogy of a cluttered room is a great expression of a human being who feels that they want to do something different and indeed deserves a change yet seems stuck in their old ways. Perhaps you simply feel that you want to empty your head of all the noise and repetitive patterns of thought which keep coming in and make you feel overwhelmed about how to make sense of things? Let me assure you that nothing will change in your life unless you change! Other family members and friends can encourage and support you in your change but no amount of telling you to change will work. You have to decide to take responsibility for your own life and be the change that you want to both see and be! Once you know this, the next step is easy.

There has never been on planet earth a better time for you to discover your own 'self-mastery'! Your own free choice is sacred. These are the rules of the puzzle of life and they come with no judgement! When you choose, however, to know more about the magnificent human being that you are, you realise that there is a grandness and beauty beyond anything that you have ever before been told.

Humanity is interconnected. We are all connected to one another through what is often referred to as the Morphogenetic Field. This word has its origins from two Greek words, 'morphine' meaning 'form' and 'genesis' meaning 'coming into being'. We cannot see this universal life force presently and nor can most of us feel it but it does exist. We each have our own unique innate intelligence structure which is responsible for our whole being. It is not restricted to our physical form and health but to our more expansive energetic and mental well-being too and which furthermore explains those individuals who experience 'spontaneous remission'.

For many it still remains a great mystery. Once the pioneering doctor who is currently inventing a quantum instrument to allow us to see this Field finishes his work, however, the surprise of everyone at observing this Field for the first time will catapult humanity's evolution beyond the leap of faith that many of us have taken to date. Each person whom we meet is effectively another soul family member. We are all members of one enormous Family of Light. There is no separation.

Confusion often comes about because we are physically living in a duality on planet earth. What does this mean? It means that there is both dark and light energy on this planet. Mother Earth, Gaia or Pachamama, by which she is also known depending on where you live, is the only planet of free choice in our galaxy at this time. The reason for the duality is so that every individual has the choice to either follow a light path or a dark path (or identify with all the vagaries that exist in between just like a plethora of make-up colours for different skin tones). As humans we are energy.

In addition to our corporeal body we have an eight metre wide field that is around us called a Merkaba or Merkabah and this is packed with over 90% of our DNA. There is non-physical DNA as well as the physical DNA in our physical body. This invisible cellular structure contains trillions of cells all acting as one. Powerful stuff! It is this Merkaba surrounding one's physical body which explains why homeopathy works and why 'spontaneous remission' works. Doctors and medical professionals listen up! It is a system of physics and not of chemistry.

In physics it is known that energy can never be destroyed. We are made up of energy. This means that we can never be destroyed. Although we die and the physical body dies, we each have a divine spark inside of us that is part of the Creator Source, God, spirit or by whatever name you want to call it. This spark of divinity within is pure and sacred. It is our soul connection and it is eternal. This explains why innately more than 80% of the world's population believes in the afterlife. There is life after death. There is life between lives. And yes, I did just write that. (As an aside, for those of you who are especially intrigued by this last sentence may I recommend Dr. Michael Newton's book titled 'The Journey of Souls').

Whether you choose to believe this or not, we keep on reincarnating on planet earth, lifetime after lifetime and the soul is truly eternal. Each time that we come back in an incarnation we pick up our accumulated wisdom from all of our past lifetimes. (For more reading on this Lady Wise refers you to her book, "Know Who You Are!").

When we choose to work in the light for our highest good (that is to be living a life filled with love, compassion, kindness, joy, abundance of everything and in harmony with nature and our surroundings) we not only raise our own 'light body', but we also in a small way positively impact the whole consciousness of planet earth by raising its level of consciousness too. This is how powerful a human being you are! It is truly beautiful! By the way, if you are interested to better understand the impact that you and everyone else is having on the consciousness of the planet right now then perhaps you may want to look up The Schumann Resonance online. This is effectively the Earth's electromagnetic pulse and it has increasingly been rising with the increased awakening of humans on this planet in alignment with their heart coherence. It was the Director, Dr. Rollin McCraty, of the HeartMath Institute Research who on explaining 'coherence' said,

"

It is a state that builds resilience – personal energy that is accumulated, not wasted – leaving more energy to manifest intentions and harmonious outcomes.

Our individual thoughts, words and actions affect this resonance measurement in Hertz not merely at a personal level but at a collective level for humanity that ripples out beyond planet earth across galaxies! After a major event in the world it will peak or trough depending on the joy or

sadness felt by everyone around the world. We are in a fast-evolving age now, dear sisters and brothers, when thankfully science is quickly catching up with esoterics. I am specifically stating this for those readers who want the science behind this esoteric content. The science of consciousness has been proven for more than 15 years and you can read more about this by looking up online The Global Consciousness Project at Princeton University, USA.

You control how fast or how slow you decide to evolve on your own path of evolution. You are the one that chooses either to bring in the beauty and the joy or alternatively the one who brings in the suffering. You create this for yourself. The Global Consciousness Project has proven that there is no such thing as luck. We are creators of our own experiences. How does that make you feel? You are your own creating creator! You are your own superhero!

From moment to moment, nano-second to nano-second, your DNA is moving and shifting depending on how you are thinking and feeling. What you think about will determine the movement of energy in your body and whether this will have a positive or negative impact on your well-being. When you choose to think more negative thoughts than positive thoughts this may be from some feelings that are unexpressed or deep thoughts that you allow to fester in your mind because you feel hard done to. The choice point is up to you!

Remember, that when you don't feel like thinking happy, joyous thoughts you can always ask for help when a situation comes along about which you are unsure what to do. I do not mean asking a friend, neighbour, work colleague or family member. I mean you can ask the creator, source, God, spirit or in whomever you believe to help you. May I suggest you make your reference point for reality to be within your heart. Each one of us is surrounded by a glorious entourage. We are born and come into this world with our own unique entourage of our guides, ancestors, angels (also referred to as Pleiadians, who are our esoteric parents) and many other energies who have only our best interest at heart. This should make you feel very proud in a humble, grateful way and encourage you to realise and understand that you are never alone.

None of us is ever alone!

As we live on planet earth in a duality, we are made to feel as if we are separate to others and alone. This is untrue. The linearity of the duality makes us feel this way. We are, however, so much more than this. We are multi-dimensional human beings living in this three dimensional reality. I am inviting you to step into your future self. Be open to new information coming your way and remember there is always a bigger picture at play!

When we start to question our own existence and increase our awareness about the soul and about our wholeness beyond our physical body, then we start to take little baby steps into the understanding that there are many realities beyond the linear reality in which most of us choose to live. This knowledge is powerful! This knowledge changes human beings and drives them to want to know more about their existence, abilities, potentials and their magnificence!

You may have heard some people talk about a 'veil'. This veil is the invisible barrier between understanding the duality and about knowing and trusting the multi-dimensional realms that exist beyond this duality to reunite you with your

wholeness. All dis-ease is merely a disconnect and imbalance with your metaphysical system of chakras on a spiritual, energetic, emotional, mental and physical level. These imbalances often have their roots in childhood from circumstances that were out with our control at that time, yet which are now outmoded for our thinking and daily living.

There is more than one reality. As you begin to ask about the puzzle of life, the multi-verse will support you in positive and benevolent change if this is what you want. There is an opportunity for every individual to reprogram the essence of who they are and correct any imbalances in their energy system to facilitate balance, good health and well-being going forward.

We are all travellers in the soul journey of life. It is indeed a puzzle but when you make a choice to ask if there is something more, then you open yourself up to unlimited possibilities of joy, love and abundance of all things from good health to money. Your life no longer needs to be a daily struggle. You wake up with a peaceful heart and trust that the universe is filled with tremendous opportunities for you. Although you may find yourself doing the same job next year as you did last year, the way you approach your job will be different. When you open your heart to the wonder of the creator source then you are saying, 'Yes' to all good things. When you expect good things to happen, they do!

When you live in harmony with everything around you, you feel freer and your heart feels lighter. The quality of the task that you are doing improves and you engage in life with joy and a sense of curiosity, aliveness and adventure. You understand and know that everyone with whom you come into contact is on their own soul journey too and you have a greater appreciation of who they are in the bigger scheme of things. You know that every encounter with another human being will change both their life and yours.

"

Consciousness has life of its own. Consciousness can pour from energy which is created from shapes.
~ Kryon

The idea of sacred geometry has been known about on this planet for a long time. Each of us is in 'a multi-dimensional soup' as Kryon calls it. In order to understand more about the mathematics and sacred geometry we require to look within ourselves and take that transformational journey into our multi-dimensionality.

A person who only thinks logical, linear thoughts is stuck in a three dimensional world. Linear thinking promotes singularity and separation. Multi-dimensional thinking, on the other hand, recognises that we all exist in a realm of wholeness, of oneness and there is no separation. Although there is no separation there remains individuation among all people. This is the essence and uniqueness of you! The other side of the veil is multi-dimensional.

Every indigenous tribe even today each has their own story of how they came to be here. Intervention is a common theme and incidentally is almost the same story as far back as research allows from both the indigenous and religious peoples.

A human being civilisation was started that was different from before because the human being's DNA was changed over a long period of time and with normal breeding, courtesy of the Pleiadian Star Mothers from the Pleiades. The human being's DNA has twenty three pairs of known chromosomes. All other animals have twenty four pairs of chromosomes. Although there is a twenty fourth pair in a human being, this is quantum and is the multi-dimensional aspect or part. It was the fusion of this twenty fourth pair by our Pleiadian Star Mothers which gave us each a piece of divinity and forever changed our existence as it had previously been – that of a human being without consciousness, without a piece of God, creator, source, spirit inside. We are born in the image of love. We are born magnificent. It is time for us to remember the core truths of the essence of our being and to live healthy lives in joy and unlimited abundance as creative source/God/spirit intended for us.

"

We are made in the image of the Creator.
~ Kryon

There is an esoteric connection to our Pleiadian parents. The Star Mothers are the parents of our soul on this planet. It never morphs. This is what it is – of purity and love.

When you break down the barrier of the veil you reunite with your helpers, your guides and your soul family. It can never be accessed when you stay in a linear frame of mind. New information is here for you to guide you on your soul journey of discovery for your highest good.

As an aside we have already witnessed how new information can influence and contribute to a change in our thinking. Take for example the exoneration of the Italian scientist and astronomer, Galileo Galilei. He had been forced by the inquisition of the Roman Catholic church back in 1633 to recant his theory that Mother Earth moves around the Sun. Although the church recognised that he had been right in 1835, it was not until more than 350 years since Galileo's persecution that Pope John Paul II finally exonerated him. To those of you reading this who already believe in reincarnation I pose the question, 'To what extent do you believe that Pope John Paul II and Sir Isaac Newton, who proved that Galileo Galilei's theory was correct, were incarnations of Galileo himself?'

Remember that we don't know what we don't know! Human beings have a tendency to put in their bias of what they know at that time. It is imperative to remember that the extent to which revealed mysteries and interpretations are explained, are only as good and as true as the maturity and raised consciousness of the individual imparting this knowledge and wisdom. A fool does not know that he is a fool. That person operating at a low level of consciousness cannot see and think higher than this level without doing the internal work on themselves to raise their vibration to a higher resonance and frequency. The ancient chakra system is one mechanism for doing this.

Kryon, whose information is based on core truths that resonate with old souls, explains to us that even Moses had perceived the creative light source to be a burning bush when he heard the creative source speak to him directly (without any 'messenger' or 'intermediary' person). Now think about this! At that time there was no electricity and the only things that would create light would have been in the sky or something burning. Today we have the science to prove that there are multiple other factors which create light. The light of the creative source would have been so pure and bright

that the highest thought and explanation that Moses would have been able to give would have been of the bush burning in front of him. All these things require to be put in perspective. We are essentially light beings of magnificence.

The science is coming when we will be able to view this light source using a quantum instrument. Oooh how that will change the way we think and perceive ourselves! It is so exciting and such an amazing adventure as humanity starts to evolve and raise their consciousness of being and understanding. There are so many things for which we cannot yet comprehend the true reasoning because we have not yet raised our vibrational frequency to that level of understanding. Sometimes we have to trust and surrender the need to know the detail.

As Kryon tells us, 'It is unimportant for you to understand the minutiae of love. Love IS!' (Or in the case of my last book, 'Love IS The Way!' Ha, ha! No plug intended. It just happened!)

The linearity in one's life always wants to know the reasons why. When as a human being we reconnect with our multi-dimensional self there is so much that we cannot understand at this time because we have not matured sufficiently within our DNA structure and our mind to be able to comprehend it. This is when I would suggest that you are courageous enough to trust in the universe in the same way that you would trust the love of your partner. Afterall, when a partner tells you that they love you, it would not be 'normal' to ask them to explain their love! Ha! Therefore, for some things the answer just 'IS'.

Who is in charge of your excuses? Simply be YOU! All you need to do is to hold the space for change to become the love that you are. There is no need to explain your thoughts and actions to anyone else. You simply trust the focus of the love vibration and belief of who you are. The shift in you will happen in divine time which incidentally may not be your time frame! Love is so powerful it magnifies the energy of everything. Perhaps you may also like to take a cleaned quartz crystal and put it under your pillow before you go to sleep at night. Quartz crystal magnifies everything that it touches and so if you expand your thinking to believe that it can magnify the love deep inside of you and that that is who you are as you are sleeping, then it will!

Remember that everyone on the planet is doing their best to learn about the power of love too, even when it looks as if they have lost their way. When you hold on to this love within, you will trigger the wondrous cellular structure that is in and around you in the Merkaba field. The trillions of DNA cells will change and start to trigger healing and good health for you. Do you appreciate that all these trillions of cells act as one? When you believe that this change is possible you are right. Similarly when you believe that this will not work you are right too! It is all about your belief. All things are possible when you believe!

Your soul waits to be aligned with the integrity of your truth. When you believe that you are indeed a magnificent human being, you have no choice but to align yourself with this core truth, to live in love every day and to honour the beauty of the amazing human being that you are, beneath all the nonsense of your mind that has had you believe that you were a victim of your life instead of being the hero and creator of your life. The ease with which you do this will keep you healthy. Remember that it is only when a person does not live in their truth that dis-ease can occur. It is your

birthright to live your life with ease and grace all the time. Is it possible that perhaps you have forgotten the importance of this statement? In the same way, it is your birthright to live in good health every day of your life.

Several years ago I met the younger sister of one of my friends. When I asked her how she was she told me that she had had an ongoing ailment that troubled her almost every day, yet she felt blessed because she enjoyed one or two days every six months when she felt ok. I explained to her that this was not normal and she looked at me completely aghast. I added that her 'normal' should be to feel good and fit every day! Perhaps that short conversation encouraged her to think differently about her own health? I'd certainly like to think so. Many individuals have become so accustomed to waking up and living in pain most days that they have momentarily forgotten that it is their birthright to live in good health every day – no excuses.

One of my passions is reiki. As a Reiki Master for more than fifteen years now, I have experience of both teaching reiki and of helping the healing journey for a variety of people and animals using reiki treatments. In this particular book, I want to explain further the chakra system which I have used to complement this healing process specifically as it applies to a human being's well-being. This non-invasive, loving, healing technique may be applied to both animals and humans, since animals have their own chakras throughout their bodies too! The focus of how this works with animals, however, will be the topic of another book which I hope to write titled 'Reiki Harmony Coupling'.

Right now it is important that you are open to understanding that you carry the energy of good health in the cells of your

energy field (Merkaba) and in the cells of your corporeal body. It is for you to know and understand that you are in control of who you are. You are all that you choose.

Why would you want to say no to good health? You are the next step to changing your body and well-being to a state of daily wellness.

I trust in you to do your part and work on yourself to make that shift to active health and wealth. When you begin to allow this thought of wellness to permeate your whole being, you will start to see subtle shift occurring to your benefit. The way you think and the way you act have a profound effect on your well-being. Those time-honoured phrases and quotes that have been passed down word-of-mouth for generations that I recall my own grand-parents speaking, for example, 'You become what you think' and 'Positive thinking will get you anywhere' are starting to have more meaning again as the new information about the power of our core being and cellular structure is not only taught esoterically but is starting to be scientifically proven.

Your wisdom is in your cellular structure.

Your Cellular Structure by Lady Wise

The vehicle in which you ride on this planet belongs to you
It is your free choice to determine how you use it and
what you do
This is the only body that you have throughout your life
So why not make the best of it with ease and grace,
banishing strife?
Until you can accept yourself and know that you're
enough

Dis-ease will linger in your field accumulating stuff
Awaken from the illusion that has you feeling sad
You have not been born a victim and for this you can be glad
It's time to honour your body and to trust in all you see
It's time to drop your karma and all dysfunctionality
You carry the energy of good health in the cells
of your innate
Which, unless activated by you as the 'Boss',
simply sit there and stagnate
So the purpose of this book is to give you guidance
on the tools
That you can use to take control without the need for
sets of rules
Take a deep nourishing breath into your heart's pulsating
sensate system
And let your soul connect with the greatness of
your inner wisdom
May your heart be as strong as your focused intention
Honour the love and support from this
two-way communication
Each time you think or speak your thoughts in a
loving, caring way
These healthy vibes positively change the cells of your DNA
With these innate instructions you enhance your intuition
Which in turn increases your awareness and expands
your inner vision
You start to get to grips with the reality of things unseen
Awakening to the truth of who you are and not whom
you have been
For when you live a love-based life as a
compassionate creator
The triad of the heart, mind and pineal gland becomes a
connecting activator

*You begin a soul journey to see that you are magnificent
in every way
There is no betrayal of anyone to dial into this
new energy today
There is no dogma, doctrine, organisation or
prescribed book
You are simply being invited to take a closer look
Your awakening on this planet affects all others when you rise
In your own consciousness from low to high, but now
comes the surprise
The science of quantum physics shows disease as a
low energy vibration
So when you are at ease and in joy, dis-ease cannot touch
you in your higher resonation.
There is no such thing as a 'high energy' disease
All disease is low energy, if you please
This means that all diseases being low energy and unable
to get to high
Are easily absorbed into a LOW ENERGY body without
instructions and these people die
You have full and total control over the healing of your
body, at a glance,
When you know you are in charge, disease does not
have a chance!
~ Lady Wise*

Science has now shown and proved that the consciousness of this planet changes physical things. This opens the door for things that have been only esoteric in the past. Free choice is absolute. Every human being is given the opportunity to question, 'Is there something more than their corporeal body?' It is about a shift in human consciousness. Remember, right now perhaps as little as 2% of the global population knows about this. This Shift is a one time only fast-track opportunity for every human being (with their free choice) to mature and accelerate to a higher kind of thinking that starts to examine itself beyond the habits and old patterns of thinking that it has had before.

"

It is a kind of thinking that raises itself up from where it was and includes things that are not necessarily part of regular thinking like the power and the result of compassion, love, fairness and kindness as a way of life. These things create an energy all of themselves that then spreads to others and it does this because the energy comes from a place that is higher than the energy from which we have come which was lower. This is enlightened thinking and has nothing to do with spirituality.
~ Kryon

What is the power behind this enlightened thinking?

All it requires from you is an open mind and an open heart to 'give it a try!' It is NOT CHEMISTRY. It is PHYSICS! This is also why homeopathy works and disappointingly, even with the recent appointment of His Royal Highness Prince Charles as a patron of the Faculty of Homeopathy (FoH) to mark the Faculty's 175th Anniversary, this healing method continues to attract angry reactions from both sceptics and academics. Allegedly one medical professional even called it 'obscene'. Sadly, such individuals are 'too smart to look' but I innately know that as you read this you know better.

There is so much benevolence, love and support for human beings at this time from the multi-verse (for we are not the only civilisation in the galaxy, albeit one of the lesser evolved civilisations). Presently, planet earth is the only planet of free choice as the rest of the universe 'watches' humanity graduate into a more mature and loving place to live. Of course we are not doing this alone. We are never alone. This is one key aspect that is fundamental for us as a civilisation to recognise and accept as we evolve in our 'knowingness' and understanding of our 'oneness'.

There is a plethora of sadness around the world simply because many people, especially elderly individuals, who are living on their own and without this knowledge believe each day that they are genuinely on their own and this is not true. Every single human being as soon as they are born on this planet has their own unique entourage of guides, ancestors, angels, whatever you want to call these beautiful essences, which, as part of the multi-verse, are with us 24/7 until we each take our last breath. This is important for those of you reading this and remembering a relative who perhaps died seemingly 'on their own' as you or another family member was unable to be with them in their last hours of physical existence.

With an increased knowledge and expansion of our wisdom, we will collectively start to consider the relevance of treating a person's health and well-being from both an holistic perspective and from that individual's personal, wholly unique experiences. No two human beings are the same, not even twins. When the Akashic record is taken into consideration which is part of the Merkaba (that eight metre coherent field that surrounds one's body) every person has had a different experience to another which has created the essence and uniqueness of who they are in this lifetime! So many health and medicine professionals have ignored the

connection of the physical body with innate (another part of the Merkaba) and so a disconnect has arisen because most people have not been given the information to enable them to understand what is going on.

The indigenous peoples have always known about this invaluable connection yet, sadly, most humans until now have ignored it because they thought they knew better. Gratefully, now that we are collectively raising our consciousness to a higher level, the increased knowledge and wisdom that is part of this higher vibration becomes recognised as a core truth of humanity. When there is belief that we are each in charge of our own cellular structure, both the visible and the invisible DNA, then we can each start to reconnect with this unifying and coherent force and begin to speak to this field as the commander, as the BOSS. As we express what we want for our physical bodies we become familiar with using the energy of consciousness to create our reality. Finally, you commence a dialogue with your body. You are talking to YOU! It is not egotistical because you are the BOSS of your own cellular structure demanding the things that it wants to hear and do! This is how you can reverse the ageing process and start youthing. Stop your ageing, slow it down and heal your body.

"

*You can slow the ageing of the body significantly by
20-30% right now with this belief system?*
~ Kryon

Every cell in your body has a unifying coherent force, so there is no need to be surprised when you have more energy! When you choose to talk to the hundreds of trillions of cells that comprise your own cellular structure they are listening to you for guidance and they all listen as one! How mind-blowing is that?

"

All it takes is for humans to be high enough in what they think, act and do with peace on earth and we will see disease like cancer disappear.
~ Kryon

Remember that all dis-ease is a low consciousness energy based on the science of quantum physics. Diseases are easily absorbed into a body that does not receive any instructions from its owner and therefore, that person will have a low energy consciousness. Every molecule , every piece of DNA in your body waits to hear from you. Your cells need direction!

When you fail to connect with your Merkaba that is part of you the cells have only one guide – the rising and the setting of the sun! All they have to do is count the days. They wait patiently for you to awaken to the power of your love within and connect with your own divine spark of spirit and magnificence. They wait for you to tell them what you want, expect and demand on a daily basis.

Since 2012, a window of opportunity and possibility was opened for us to see the puzzle of life in a different way. What are the energies that we are experiencing now? We are moving into a New Earth that is experiencing more light on the planet than there has been for eons. As Earth spends the next ten years passing through these final years of the thirty-six year Precession of the Equinoxes cycle, everything is becoming unpredictable. Why? The reason is because Gaia

has never been on this elliptical path before as humanity experiences a rapid awakening i.e. a transcendence of duality into multi-dimensionality. Everything comes from the light, even darkness. Have you noticed that everything is drawn to the light, especially insects when one is camping out with only a torch! Ha! Regardless of how ugly the dark can be, the dark is part of the light too. The planet is undergoing a test of light and dark energies. It's time to mature and wise up to who you are and to humanity's evolution of life!

Love is pure. Love has no doctrine. Love exists and following love is the way for you to see the love of your soul. Across the globe humans are asking questions about the puzzle. What is essential for your life?

Today in this new energy many of us are starting to see things from a different perspective than before. So many processes, systems, rules and procedures are looking dysfunctional. All of a sudden everything looks dysfunctional. This is what evolution is about. It is as if a light is suddenly being turned on and we are observing and thinking about things that we never gave a second thought to before. Are you chasing money in your career or are you passionate about chasing your purpose in life and what you love to do?

The new energy on this planet is indeed filled with more light than darkness which is why we are able to evolve as a civilisation. It is time to start looking for the love and integrity in all things once more like we first did when those of us as 'old souls' were present on Lemuria.

When we reconnect with our entourage and with the love of the creator, source, God, spirit in our hearts everything starts to make sense. As each human being awakens to the magnificence of who they are, their awakening not only affects them in a personal way but because we are all connected it also affects the collective consciousness on planet earth and throughout many galaxies.

Consciousness creates invention, high consciousness creates high invention and more!
~ Kryon

The efficiency of your health, your DNA and your physical body is linked to your consciousness level. What you believe is what you will become. Did you know that DNA is built to last almost nine hundred years? When there is a higher consciousness level attained on Gaia as a result of more compassion, understanding and peace on earth there will be longer life experienced by so many more. First, however, it is up to each of us to choose to reconnect with our cellular structure, reconnect with our own divinity and celebrate these wonders of human life!

Mother Earth, Gaia, Pachamama is destined for a future of high, high consciousness, just as our esoteric parents the Pleiadians have already achieved this on the Pleiades.

Know that all of your life experiences to date including any failure or disappointment in your life have brought you one step closer to love, joy and unlimited abundance!

We have a remarkable new energy in which to create something different. The planetary energies presently are encouraging us to spread our wings and become more adaptable and flexible about what we do and the adventure in our life. Humanity is slowly starting to become more conscious of the duality on planet earth in all its different

forms not just in the outside world but also of our inner world and our body. We never forget to breathe and yet how often do we express gratitude for the work that our lungs do?

How easily can you adapt to a change in circumstances? How flexible can you be after receiving a disappointment? Remember there are different types of flexibility to consider. There is emotional flexibility, mental flexibility as well as physical flexibility of which to be aware.

Grief is often an emotion which can trap an individual for years because they are unable to rise above this. As we come to an understanding that our past memories and experiences are not who we are today, although they have enabled us to reach this place in this moment, we are able to honour these aspects of our life and accept that the purpose of our life is not to hold on to this grief. In this awareness and maturity about life, we find a way to release these emotions and feel a freedom that comes with this that makes us feel lighter and able to surrender to something that is so much bigger than ourselves.

In truth, each of us has experienced difficult places in our lives when after having tried all that we know how we simply need help from that something more, that something bigger. By whatever name you honour this energy, this force, God, spirit, the creator source, it sits and waits patiently for us to surrender and allow it to come into our lives and makes us feel loved beyond measure. There is no exclusion. We are all connected. We are all dearly loved by the universe but the free choice that we have been given means that WE HAVE TO ASK FOR HELP.

Remember free choice is absolute. So if you are feeling that you don't know what to do anymore or you know someone who is experiencing challenges at this time may I suggest you reach out to them and offer this guidance. This may be the healing that you or a friend has been waiting for, longing for to turn around their life in a more positive way. Consciousness is that mysterious, invisible energy that is all around you and in you.

Consciousness is energy –
it does not follow linearity and
it is ready to be shared
~ Kryon

You are always loved until your last breath. The more you start to study the energy of consciousness the more you start to realise this is the way it is. How truly awesome this is! You are never alone.

The evolving human spirit understands the vastness of this consciousness, the vastness of all that is which is different from what we were originally told. For example, reincarnation was included as part of the Christian faith until the sixth century when it was taken out, perhaps for political reasons? Start thinking for yourself in terms of what it would mean to a dynasty, such as the Romans, who may not have been able to control the people as well had they been without the 'whip of Judgement Day' under which to keep the masses suppressed and repressed? Interestingly enough across many other religions of which I am only going to name a few such as Buddhism, Hinduism, Islam , Judaism, and Sufi traditions, reincarnation is included as part of these religious and historic cultures.

The benevolent energy of consciousness is everywhere. It is available for everyone. There is no 'interim messenger'

required to come between you and this energy. It is a loving energy that knows no exclusions. It is not religious. This means that you do not go to a specific location or place of worship and then return home.

When I was 12 years old I would wonder why people would go to church every Sunday dressed up in their 'Sunday Best' (myself included at this time as I remember with fondness my teal coloured wool caped coat which came down to my mid-calf and was really warm in winter), sit and listen to the Minister give his sermon, sing hymns and be most polite with those around them until they had shaken the hand of the minister on exiting the church, only to then go and gossip the rest of the week about other people. It seemed very insincere to me.

Your soul is from the creative soul – there is no separation! This is what makes you magnificent! You are so worthy of receiving love from your creator as you in turn would love your children. Human beings have put up the barriers to this pure truth themselves. Now is the time to recognise in the depths of your soul that this is indeed a core truth. Feel it resonating in your heart.

Often there is no reason to change unless something happens. Generally, humans do not like change. They are reluctant to embrace change. With the current health challenges across the globe there is a health crisis, economic crisis and financial crisis. The light that will come from this will be that of hope, trust and compassion. Individuals are being forced into scenarios to innovate and create new ways of doing things.

For example, we have already seen the Mercedes Formula 1 team rise to the challenge to design ventilator equipment that was considered necessary and appropriate as their

contribution to saving lives during the early recognition of the coronavirus pandemic. One personal trainer in England has been helping to deliver food to the elderly. A Japanese whisky company has been using their American subsidiaries to produce bottles of sanitiser fluid for those people working in the health services and police. The list is endless and the selflessness of individuals involved is humbling. This is demonstrative of the new paradigm of humans who are maturing and evolving on this planet with love at the heart of what they do. How refreshing this is and how wonderful that such COMPASSIONATE ACTION IS INFECTIOUS!

The choice point for you is very simple. Do you want to live a life in love or do you want to live a life based in fear? This is the paradigm shift. Fear, worry, stress and anxiety stop the light penetrating your cellular structure and your chakra system. When you decide to let the light flow through you and relax into your body safe in the knowledge that you are known by the universe, you are supported for your highest good to build a life filled with togetherness and love.

I find it very comforting to know that each of us is filled with the healing power of love and every day when we show compassion for others that generates wonderful light. The more love and compassion that we have, the more our light force within cooperates with our cellular structure and gives us good health.

"

You are not alone if you question the things
that are sacred within you.
~Kryon

How do you power up on a higher consciousness? When you quiet your mind and listen to the messages from your intuition, from meditation or sit quietly listening to your favourite music, for example, it feels like you are in another reality and of course, you are. Moreover, when you are able to stay open to a higher perspective that always has your highest good at the heart of the matter then you can let yourself sink down into your heart chakra and truly feel the love of the benevolent energies all around you. You can invite a part of this consciousness to stay with you – this is what you came for – and then carry it around with you wherever you go. This is the feeling that you keep in your body as evolved consciousness.

In this new energy of this new earth that we are just beginning to see since 2012, we are now in a fast-track period of time to allow our own spiritual rebirthing.

"

This creative source of love from the universe is not a judgemental God. This is not a God that gives you complete free choice and then judges you on your choice.
~ Kryon

The wisdom of all the Masters who have been and who are on this planet has never been properly understood because the consciousness of human beings has previously always been so low energetically that they put the creator source, spirit, God, by whatever name one would call this creative energy, on a pedestal. What has been forgotten is that the Masters came to show us and have us emulate them. We are a part of God not apart from God!

The heart coherence that you feel when you are in a group of collected 'old souls' starts to pave the path for a new earth, for a new consciousness where higher thinking brings about new solutions, co-creations and collaborations to lift humanity into a new paradigm where compassion, kindness and love are cool. Instead of the old paradigm of being perceived as showing weakness, love and compassion in this new world now express only strength and blessed qualities of patience, understanding, kindness and forgiveness.

Although there are many kinds of energies on the planet, as a metaphysical person I consider there are mainly two kinds – light and dark. The duality of light and dark energy is starting to shift on this planet. In this duality, the dark and light balance or quotient of dark and light is starting to move increasingly towards the light. What does this mean? Light is responsible for a consciousness that starts to clean up things that have always been the same for hundreds of years. It shines on dark places where there has been a lack of integrity, corruption, abuse of power and low energy consciousness. It is meant to show you what you didn't see before. This was the prediction of the ancients when they spoke of a calendar and of a 'wobble of the earth' that they called the Precession of the Equinoxes. So many of them drew a demarcation point of energy stating that past this Shift, if we would make it, consciousness would have an opportunity to become higher. Essentially, a consciousness of higher thinking by humanity with love as its core truth would evolve. This is what is happening now. The landscape has changed forever. Of these two principal kinds of energies, linear (dark) energy and non-linear (light) energy one of them is going to occur more often than the other. And guess what? Light is winning!

Now it becomes more interesting! Anything that is common and known conforms to the law of the inverse square (how distance affects transmission), but this is linear! Metaphysical people have dealt with energies that were not linear for thousands of years. Healing energy that works and can be counted on, on a regular basis, such as reiki, is an example of this. I have been a Reiki Master since 2003. It is somewhat mysterious because the energy cannot be seen by the physical eye and yet, from my own experiences with both people and animals it offers great healing to them both when I am present with the receiver and when I am using distance healing across thousands of miles to the beneficiary of the reiki. I am dealing with a bias. A bias is what one is used to because it works. To you, it may be an aspect of what you learned in school perhaps. It then becomes your reality and this then becomes your bias. Yet, when you are shown something outside of this bias, you may still be unsure and suspect of it. Now is the time to be curious, to stay inquisitive and to learn more about how to become more open in your heart and engaged with the new information, ideas and solutions that are coming in to help us individually and collectively raise our vibrational frequency to hold more light, love, knowledge and wisdom.

Multi-dimensional energy was first looked at and discovered by physicists (quantum physicists) more than fifty years ago. One of Albert Einstein's dreams was to find a formula for everything. When the multi-dimensional experiments began there was a series of debates between him and those physicists who identified that some things did not respond to rules. Light was one such thing. Light is multi-dimensional.

*Entanglement is the closest thing to what the
Hindus believe – one with everything. In this case,
Einstein labelled this as 'spooky action at a distance'*
~ Kryon

When twins can feel each other's pain or joy, for example, across thousands of miles this is outside of linearity that has energy that can be predicted. Healers use this type of energy. The healers in Egypt used it – it is not new! Disappointingly for years, culturally much of humanity has been talked out of it. Now it is all beginning to change as more and more people better understand the science of energy.

There are certain emotions of consciousness that create an amplification. It has not been measured yet but we can start to FEEL it. Compassion, love, kindness, patience, oneness starts to have a confluence when put together with different human beings in a room. It is almost like a node is created that changes the energy around it and amplifies it.

*Two or three people together with the same kind of energy,
however, will not merely create the amplification of two
or three. Instead, it becomes more like a hundred!
It is way beyond linearity.*
~ Kryon

These energies, which in the past have been deemed mystical, are actually energies of love, compassion and kindness. It is about the compassion for one another. Very soon this will be able to be measured. This is new energy on the planet that is starting to show itself. This multi-dimensional energy of which Kryon speaks is an evolutionary energy. Eventually the experiments will reveal that the new amplifier is compassion. Compassionate action creates a field that everybody else knows what is going on. The ancient Egyptians knew about this and counted on it.

Ponder the beauty that is all around you, above you, beneath your feet, to your left, to your right, to your front and to your back – ponder the free things that are there for you – free air, free birdsong, free butterflies, insects and bees, flowers, plants, wild animals and trees to name but a few.

LOVE IS NOT EMOTION, IT IS COMMUNICATION. IT IS TWO-WAY COMMUNICATION WITH THE CREATOR. The most basic form of this is intuition. It is one of the hardest things to be able to describe and yet once you understand this communication to the other side of the veil then when you are quiet, your intuition is able to show itself to you in a more profound and deeper way.

Be still and embrace the experience of sitting in the silence of the void between you and your creator! One solution is to find out the truth for yourself when you listen to yourself! Every one of us is capable of receiving great inspiration and integrating this at many levels to achieve an expansive perspective of what is true. Furthermore, this exercise will help you to determine what you intentionally want to develop with confidence and success in your life.

When you feel the communication from that something that is so much bigger than you it is not a one-way communication. The two-way communication is not linear. It is love. Love is quantum.

Two-way communication is the way of it.
The essence of God is love.
~ Kryon

You can feel that you are connected when you sit quietly in combination with your intuition. As Kryon states it is very difficult to define. Most of us have 'intuitive flashes' simply because they come and go so fleetingly. Within this intuition there is a spark of multi-dimensional consciousness that communicates with spirit. For example, just think about when you have an intuitive thought to do something. Without changing it at all, trust that first intuitive thought for this is accurate and true. Sometimes the intuitive thought can come across as a picture and this becomes a catalyst for the next stage in your journey of self-discovery.

Think of intuition as tuning into the right frequency for you to receive what it is you need to know that will support and guide you for your highest good.

What brings you joy into this world? This will help to centre you. It will also raise your vibration, which will enhance your intuition and support you in connecting better to the universe, creative source, God, spirit. How different would the world be when we each live in joy? You are a part of the shifting energy in these Changeover Years. When you deny yourself the joy that is your birthright, you are stifling your light, your connection to source and suppressing your self-esteem and self worth to be the essence of whom you are.

History is not going to repeat itself! Wake up!

All the children who have been born after 21 December 2012 are reincarnating on planet earth and come in knowing who they are without the prejudice of old energy patterning and the history of wars on Mother Earth. Instead, they come in knowing that they have a purpose and that there is purpose to everything that happens, even when this means that some human beings die early as compassionate souls leaving behind loved-ones who are sorrowful, only to reincarnate once again and become even grander in their evolutionary humanitarian pursuits.

We came to this planet to be part of an elegant earth for an evolvement of humanity. It is about individual consciousness of compassionate care for human beings. There is no dogma or doctrine but a genuine generic paradigm of caring. This is the essence of peace on earth and as more and more human beings mature in their knowingness and consciousness, the closer we come to achieving this.

Women are naturally the life-givers and compassionate ones and these are the reasons women tend to make better leaders and shamans. They have the inbuilt compassion that they would use to rear their children. They have a greater ability to listen in love. Such beautiful guidance comes from the female who is so loving, kind, patient and compassionate.

No-one was born to be a victim. Each human being has been born to be part of something that is beautiful. This is the Shift. Human nature is changing albeit slower than the 'old souls' would like for we know what is coming and we can metaphorically 'smell and taste' peace on earth! Ha! Ha!

You are designing your reality. You with consciousness have control of chance! Did you know that consciousness can change the numbers that come up on a dice? Disappointingly, there are those human beings who still think that luck is the basis of life. People will believe what they want to believe and that is perfectly valid. It is their free choice.

The reality you create outside of chance puts you together with others who are creating the same thing such as a desire for peace on earth.

"

Do not buy in to anyone who says luck controls your life!
You control it with consciousness, right place, right time.
~ Kryon

It has to do with higher thinking, with consciousness and a belief system that we can control our own reality. It is an invitation for synchronicity. It has nothing to do with religion.

All that you have ever wanted for you and your family you can start to control.

This is such vital information for you to know and understand that I have also composed a song about this in the hope that if my written words do not inspire you then perhaps my musical version with lyrics will!

The universe is helping to jolt us into remembering the magnificence of the dearth of possibilities and potentials that are available to us when we decide to connect to the cosmic intelligent force field and live a love based life. Do you know what if feels like to truly be yourself? Can you see a healthy sense of self when you look in the mirror? There is no need to always figure out everything yourself when you have your own personal entourage to support you even when you are sleeping! May I suggest that you

stay open to what you cannot see coming that has only your highest good at heart?

New timelines and pathways become available to you when you are willing to open up to how wonderful your future can be. Can you trust yourself and the universe to step away from what has not been working for you and the three dimensional matrix of linear life and step out into a brave new world that you are actively creating every day when you embrace a new way of understanding the puzzle of life and your 'hero' role as the creator of it? How do you show up in the world?

There is every reason to enjoy each day in joy and hope. New solutions are on their way! Saturn's conjunction with Aquarius in October 2020 triggered many new ideas and fresh concepts as we get past the vulnerability and emotions of what has recently occurred. The quicker you are able to face the truths, acknowledge and understand what has been and is happening, the easier it will be for you to adapt to the changes that will be necessary to go forward as you rebuild stronger foundations for yourself on a personal level and address what is needed for your family, relationships, finances, home, career and your business/work to be successful in a more loving and compassionate way.

We are at the start of a whole new decade and when we accept these challenges we not only open our mind and heart to living a life with greater ease and grace, but we learn and grow in our spiritual development. The astronomical and astrological impact of the Capricorn Stellium on 12 January 2020, about which much knowledge has been imparted by those more learned on these matters than myself, has initiated energies that will have major implications for humanity

across the next three decades! These BIG energies are heralding permanent change. Nothing is permanent. Change is constant. Most humans do not like change. We are moving into new beginnings at a global and local level that demand integrity, truth and love as their foundation attributes. At the personal level, it is about questioning the integrity of our own belief system and understanding that good things take time to achieve, even in an uncertain climate.

These are truly auspicious times when we can learn to relax and go with the flow of the adventure of life in harmony and balance as we get to know ourselves better in this lifetime.

"

Always know you are loved by the creator source
Regardless of your circumstances and quotient of
light force
There is no reason to feel a need to cling to anyone
or material things
For you are continually guided and protected with
angels' wings
Instead of venting feelings of anger in frustration
Contain this energy within and transmute it
Into focused contemplation
Allow emotions on the issue to dissolve on this occasion
Find the most mature solution with balance and
practical consideration
Let life flow through you and stay strong in your essence
Learn to manage your energy day-to-day with
confidence and presence.
~ Lady Wise

CHAPTER 2

The Energy of YOU!

When you can learn to master your inner power
Your intuition, heart and pituitary gland as one will flower
Such knowledge and abundance will make you feel blessed
You are the ultimate authority on what you choose to do next!
~ Lady Wise

Welcome to the world of metaphysics and to the energy of YOU! How beautiful it is to connect to heart coherence! After a tired mind following a day's hard work it may often seem inappropriate to spend time sitting down quietly and caring for one's heart. What difference would that make? All the difference to the world and more importantly all the difference to YOU!

Our beautiful heart keeps us alive with every bountiful beating heartbeat, filled with compassion and love for us as we exist and live in this temporary physical body. We are spirit. This is innate. We are of a higher power when we close down our logical minds and allow the sacredness of

love to flow in to our spiritual beingness. Our heart has always known that we were connected. At a deep level we have known that we are connected to something so much bigger than ourselves. This is the Shift. It is the shift in understanding of our being. This is the evolution of humanity and it will become revelationary to so many over the coming decade as we drop the fakery, falsenesss, illusion, delusion, confusion and deception that has been prevalent across so many mediums including selective social media, television and newspapers. It is time to draw back and turn inwards for a visionary insight into the essence of who we are and to our existence and the aliveness that can come from this which is our birthright. There is much confusion about our purpose on Mother Earth. Each one of us is here for a reason even although we may not know why at this time.

When you take your last breath you simply change form. You do not die when your physical body dies, because you are not your body. Many of you reading this may previously have heard of the quote from the theologian, Teilhard de Chardin,

"

We are not human beings having a spiritual experience.
We are spiritual beings having a human experience.

There is an energy that connects all of us. The essence of who we truly are as a divine piece of the creator source is this connector. This inherently means that we are all creators.

"

When you create, create, create
You cannot make a mistake!
~ Lady Wise

How many of you feel lit up inside when you work on a creative project? Do you feel a real sense of passion, instinct and enthusiasm when you take time to think about a new creative idea? All this creativity requires the bringing together of beautiful, uplifting fire energy. Whether these successes are on a small or a large scale, the love that you put into creating and manifesting them enables you to work in a multi-dimensional state that is free from judgement, free from competition and indeed allows a healthy flow of your energy throughout your body as you focus on beauty and pleasure. At both a conscious and unconscious level by rechannelling your energy into doing what you love, your heart is being strengthened and you are being awakened in the process to a greater infinite understanding of life in the universe.

Remember, health issues always show up where there is no flow of life force energy throughout your body with ease and grace. It is important for you to feel strong in whatever you are doing and to take care of yourself. You may find the easiest way to do this is by introducing a daily routine and/or devotion related to exercise, food, meditation, singing, dancing, walking, bathing in essential oils, whatever you need to do when you show up every day to ensure that you are taking care of your body and are supporting the energy flow through your 'energy container' to support it in all you do.

We must never forget that we always have a choice in everything we do. No excuses! Unless you train your mind to be your servant and not your master, it will always find excuses that will keep you feeling trapped and controlled in awkward circumstances but whenever you can find that inner strength and courage to make a different choice that is always focused on your highest good and the highest good of the universe, you will be supported by the most wonderful,

beautiful invisible energies who are always with you and want the best life for you, at your request.

The energy that is you takes on different meanings in your life. There is the energy that runs through you at a very personal, intimate, sacred level which honours your inner world and the energy within you that you then use to connect and engage with others in the outer world. All of this energy of you is important in shaping more about who you are and in helping you to progress your soul growth in this lifetime.

Perhaps the most obvious visible energy about you is your body and physical appearance. When you look in the mirror and take a close look at yourself it is important to truly have a sense of who you are and of your personal appearance. Do you LOVE what you see? If yes, this is wonderful news. Equally, if you are a person who feels nauseated looking in the mirror and who takes a dislike to certain body parts that are all part of you, incidentally, then we have a little more work to do. All is well! You are just as magnificent a being as everyone else around you right now. You simply need to believe this and stop comparing yourself to others. You have so much talent and gifts, some of them hidden presently, about which your conscious mind does not know but your innate knows all about. When you can take a close look at yourself with all your 'perceived' imperfections (because spirit always sees you as perfect) and laugh about the fact that there is so much more to you than what you look like then you have reached a positive tipping point in your life and there will be no going back!

Here is a little poem that I wrote several years ago now as a reminder of the humour that we can bring to our physical appearance.

A REALITY CHECK

O mirror, mirror on the wall, that's not the person I recall!
The zipper strains, the waistband pinches, what can be done
to reduce the inches?
With my ego punctured, my confidence deflated; if I was
more streamlined I would be elated
A little past my sell by date, I need some help to rejuvenate
Having worked, wed, bred, and become somewhat jaded,
would a spa weekend revive what has faded?
While relaxing, yet bracing, a wellness régime means good-bye
depression and 'hello self-esteem!'
Such a wonderful stay in a stress-free zone would give me
plenty of time for a body tone
As well as enjoying a complete overhaul, I could practice my
favourite butterfly, backstroke and crawl
Being pampered to perfection, I would gladly look at my
radiant reflection
No more fat tums and podgy thighs, only a healthy lifestyle
regimen including exercise
So having accepted that I am not bionic, I give up my
favourite gin and tonic
I indulge in a Crystal Steam Room treat at Stobo Castle's
luxurious retreat
Opting for brie tart, fresh berries and celery sticks, there is
no further need for a high glucose fix
Now happily facing the big 'five-o', I emerge refreshed and
raring to go!

The power of nature is terrific for restoring our va va voom
and for attaining that wonderful glow to the skin that makes
us feel more healthy and comfortable in our skin. Our vehicle
or vessel is carried with us for life and when you are critical

of your own body then you dampen and dull your beautiful auric field that surrounds your physical body. You dull your own light that is the essence of you because you are essentially stifling your happiness and joy that radiates from you and to all who are receptive to your energy.

You are your own power house and the best person to brighten up your day with sunshine is YOU! Acceptance of who you are now and how your physical body looks and feels to you now is key to retaining your own personal power. Yes of course natural improvements and refinements can be made without surgery if you really want to make some changes but the ease and grace with which this will happen for you starts with you accepting you NOW...as you are! When you have the awareness to be accepting of all of you regardless of any subtle physical changes that you want to make, then you start to fall into alignment with your true sense of self and your creative power. With grace and insight your own physical body will make the changes you want to see without struggle, hard work and effort. Your own innate knows what you need and what you want without you having to work in isolation from these hundreds of trillions of non-physical multi-dimensional DNA cells. You can learn to be graceful in your actions and to speak kindly to yourself which are the ingredients for a physical body transformation.

Moreover, when you strive for more awareness about how you are your own person, you will build up more inner strength to make wise decisions for yourself and embrace the opportunity of loving life with a heart that is free from an enslaved destiny.

Loving and accepting yourself as is will greatly support your own frequency level and improve your self-confidence, self-worth and self-esteem. It is only ourselves who can weaken our own power when we feel so unsure of who we are that we give away our power to other individuals, often without realising this act. No-one can take away your own power without your permission. Many of us require to check in with our own insight, self-knowledge and awareness to realise and understand this.

It is so important to be gentle with yourself in learning how to get to the root of a personal experience that has made you feel down-trodden or worthless so that this pattern is not repeated. When you are able to identify with these types of situations that have happened to you in the past then they can be healed and you can move through the heart issue without fear of this old program recurring in the future. Belief in this itself is very liberating and empowering which is all part of learning about our own energy and how to control it for our highest good and for our spiritual growth in this lifetime.

As we learn to become self-reliant and listen to the messages that all our senses share with us, we begin to live a life that is more in keeping with our truth and our own uniqueness. Furthermore, we start to establish and manifest scenarios that enable us to support our own frequency across our relationships, family, career, finances, property and home matters and material possessions. The trigger points for allowing a greater harmonious and fulfilled life to be enjoyed become a self-fulfilling prophecy of abundance, joy and love. The more that one's frequency is independently nurtured and supported, the more confidence that is self-generated which raises one's vibration to attract and enable higher levels of thinking. These thoughts, each being a unit of consciousness, in turn, produce those higher innovative and creative

solutions. The ability to harness one's creative power brings an efficiency of purpose to the individual which focuses their actions and blesses them with loving fulfilment. An extension of this quantum mindset would then inspire that individual to work for the good of others as well as for themselves.

The magic of your energetic is that it touches everyone else whom you meet who is receptive to your radiating creativity and awareness. How cool is that? You, by being true to you, influence everyone else around you who chooses to be receptive to your own energy. This is how collectively we can rise in our energetic vibration. As we each rise in our own knowledge of understanding about ourselves, we give permission for those with whom we connect and communicate to rise in their own understanding of who they are too! It is infectious positive energy of pure love! Awesome!

So when we have this awareness of our own power how effectively do we communicate, share, receive and teach it to others? The way that you perceive your own energy and understand the ways of the universe and your specialness in it, will determine how you think, learn, understand, organise and communicate to the world around you. How you use your powers of communication in the outer world will drive the enhancement and expansion of your own inner mind.

For example, when you are always consciously aware of communicating with others in a clear way to avoid misinterpretation by others of what you say and you do this for the highest good of the situation, then you will be rewarded with a reconnection of non-physical DNA and neural pathways that were previously shut down in prior lifetimes. It is possible in this lifetime to open up the efficiency of one's pineal gland which, when linked to the heart and

to the mind, activates an improvement in one's quantum abilities. This is directly linked to your ability to honour, let go and release old patterning and programming about which you were told when you were younger and which has now been superseded with new information, some of which I am sharing with you in this book and other esoteric books that I have written.

Throughout all of this exploration of self, it is fundamental that you can feel safe, grounded and strong in everything that you are doing. The ease with which you feel at home on this planet and inspired by the unlimited abundance of love that is available to support you in all ways, opens the door, metaphorically, of how you, of your choosing, fast-track your quest for good health, intuitive strength and wisdom.

Each of us needs a space to go where we can feel alone to 'just be'. Make sure you give yourself this gift of a space, no matter how small, and honour yourself with a little private time to reflect, give gratitude and consolidate your thoughts of what you want to achieve in your life and how you want to nurture yourself at a soul level to feel nourished and fulfilled in your life. Remember that this privacy does not have to be shared with anyone else because it is an opportunity for you to regularly check in with whom you are and with whom you are becoming in the environment of the sacredness of your own being. It is you with you! As a suggestion you may like to use some of this 'soul time' to better understand your heart matters and to listen to your intuition for what feels right as next steps. You may feel that you want to connect with the creative source, God, spirit or by whatever name you give this energy, for a whole variety of reasons such as:-

- to feel inspired in your thinking;

- to receive the gift of greater patience regarding a particular matter;

- to manage frustration and anxieties about an outcome that has yet to conclude;

- to seek safety and protection in all your travels;

- to trust your feelings more;

- to receive enhanced intuition;

- to practice stronger heart coherence.

These lists are endless but when you quiet your mind you will know what you need for your highest good at that time to give you peace of mind and a feeling of balance with all that is.

When we live from a place of joy and love in our heart and can see beauty in all things then we also enhance our psychic abilities. And yes, everyone is psychic whether they believe it or not. Ha!

One of the best ways to experience more of who we are is to remember to have fun! When was the last time that you laughed so much it made your stomach ache? When did you last eat an ice-cream cone, go down a shoot or ride a donkey as examples? In Japan, one company chief executive listened to his employees and adopted the idea of one of them to build a full size shoot in the office to aid as a stress buster. The employee who suggested this was very surprised when the owner agreed. Now everyone in the office can enjoy having fun at work! Moreover, this owner's passion for helping others guided him to build exact replicas of patients' hearts which are in need of major surgery using a

stereolithography 3D printer. This ground-breaking achievement enables an initial model heart complete with the insides to be made within four days of an original CT scan. Such a model is of a material structure which allows incisions and stitches to be done. This means that surgeons can practice major heart surgery before working on the patient's real heart. It has directly instilled greater confidence in surgeons than ever before and shaves on average a valuable forty minutes off the live surgery. Many children in need of heart surgery have reaped the benefit from this practice.

What makes you feel alive, happy and fully in your power? Your ability to have fun actually stimulates your creativity and gives you clarity of mind. There was a NASA creativity experiment undertaken involving approximately 1,600 children. The test outcome demonstrated that our creativity is blatantly not encouraged as we age as follows:-

Age	Creativity Percentage
4 – 5 years	98%
10 years	30%
15 years	12%
31 years	2%

Is it any wonder that so many adults feel discombobulated at age thirty? They are depriving themselves of effervescence and light force which is at the core of their 'energy body'. We are meant to live fully as beings of light, as creators of our world, uninhibited from anything, even our imagination!

So how can we increase our creativity? How much do you really want to? Remember you have full creative control and so even a simple ten minutes time out every day with a blank canvas (loosely referring to paper, tablet screen, chalk board, art canvas or the back of an envelope) perhaps you may feel like doodling, making up words, writing down a poem or lyrics for a song. I would also encourage you to look in your wardrobe and be creative with any old garment that you really like but which is a little tired looking and in need of a style boost. Sometimes a change of buttons or a change in sleeve length from long to three quarters for example is enough to make you feel good wearing it again. For those who are more daring perhaps a change in colour of a garment would enliven it. Careful though because fabrics all work in different ways with dye and I would not want you to go ahead gung-ho without seeking professional advice first! Simple trims that are detachable can make a difference to the overall look when styling a garment too!

In your home you can move around furniture and paintings to create a different ambience in a room. Consider introducing different plants and flowers to your home both indoors and outdoors to stimulate your mind to think differently. In this way you also receive the benefit from the oxygen they give out and they receive the benefit from breathing in the carbon dioxide you exhale.

Next time you go shopping consider looking at items in a different way. Perhaps there is an object sold as a lunchbox that would make a great toilet bag, a utensil holder that would be perfect as a crayon holder, children's wooden name initial door letters collated to form an affirmation reminder on your desk or wall. Literally taking a step back in a shop from the various shelves and rails can open your heart and mind to a different perspective. I dare you to do this and see how creative you can become! Observe the change in

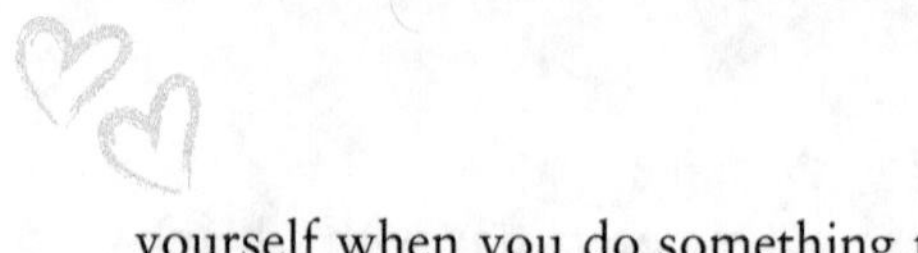

yourself when you do something that makes you experience and feel sensations in a new place of power.

How can you feel more confident and healthy in everything you do? In order to have a strengthened immune system and to optimise your health and well-being, it is important for you to address what care you require to give yourself on a daily basis. Virgo season is especially ripe for this because one aspect of Virgo focuses on the intention that we give to our body working at the physical level to ensure that our meridians are clear and flowing properly around our circulatory system. I can give you a few tips but each one of us is so unique that you can have fun finding out what best resonates with your body. Everyone has their own beliefs about what works for them. For example, many individuals benefit from acupuncture, hot stone therapy, reiki, foot massage, hand massage, facial and body massages. Here is a few other suggestions for you to follow up on as you wish. Beautiful essential oils can be used as part of bathing, as part of a massage routine for grounding your body, as a room fragrance as well as specifically contributing to the treatment of certain ailments.

Base Note Oils

Aromatherapy base note oils to which you can refer
Are Ylang Ylang, Sandalwood, Parsley, Myrrh
Aniseed, Benzoin, Cinnamon, Clove,
Cypress, Fennel, Frankincense, Rose,
Black Pepper, Nutmeg, Ginger, Neroli,
Cardamom, Cedarwood, Jasmine and Patchouli.
Let cinnamon's spicy massage oil leave you in warming
mood

*While jasmine's floral fragrance has you energised and
feeling good
A massage with black pepper is great to conquer muscle
spasm
Ginger compress is comforting and can fill a healing
chasm
Clove skin care helps with respiratory infection
Bath time with frankincense delivers calming reflection
Aniseed produces a relaxing feeling aiding flatulence and
indigestion
Sandalwood as a cream compress is soothing for insomnia
protection
The woody scent of benzoin treats throat infections and
skin irritations
Fennel skin care energises one's body and can also be
taken via inhalation
Patchouli used in massage is best for damaged skin
Exotic ylang ylang is brilliant to avoid stress setting in
Menstrual disorders are helped by inhaling smoky
myrrh
A soothing cedarwood massage eases eczema and acne
that occur
Parsley refreshes one's emotions and can stimulate
circulation
Fresh cypress oil is a natural disinfectant, eases digestion
and wonderful for rejuvenation
Spicy nutmeg oil has warming properties good for
tired muscles
Rich, floral neroli inhaled may leave you with euphoric
corpuscles!
Cardamom oil treats rheumatic aches and arthritis well
While the delicate sweet, rose oil is uplifting just by
its smell.*

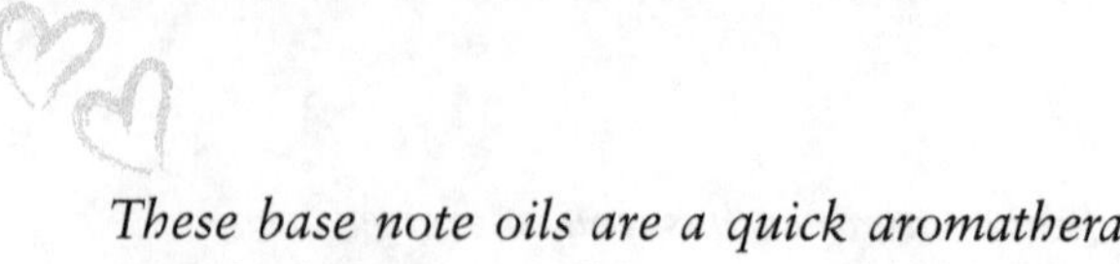

Vitamins may help to strengthen your 'energy body' especially as so much agricultural soil has been weakened from exposure to chemical fertilisers.

As an aside, with all the chaotic weather patterns around the world it is easy to become caught up in the fear and worry of it all. I want to reassure you that all is well. This climate cycle would have happened without humanity living on Mother Earth, Pachamama or Gaia. The weather pattern changes have been known about for more than a decade and moreover, there are those scientists such as Gregg Braden who understand that the present timeframe is required to allow Mother Earth to recalibrate after the marker of 21 December 2012, when humanity was mid-stream in the Precession of the Equinoxes and on its way to graduate status as a planet. Mother Earth is watched patiently by those who seeded us almost 30,000 years earlier. The wonderful aspect to all this is that beyond duality or three dimensional logical thinking there is no time and space. It is time for us to awaken to the truth about our existence and reconnect with our multi-dimensionality.

"

The truth of history changes with discovery.
~ Kryon

All energies are thriving in quantum dimensions and so although they have waited patiently they have not seemed to have waited as long as one might think. For eons, human beings have had a tendency to think too much instead of letting themselves go with the flow of their daily lives – letting themselves open up to adventures – whether this is meeting new people as they travel the same road to work every day or whether this is travelling to different places and seeking out new friends and acquaintances from such an activity. Throughout all of life it is so important for each of us to trust ourselves and thoughts and not to be dissuaded by others when it comes to manifesting our dreams.

Taking time to stand still sit peacefully and quietly in contemplative creation is a special time. Inward introspection allows us to open up our heart to greater clarity and intuitive thought directly from the creator source. This is how Albert Einstein, Nikola Tesla and many classical composers sourced their innovations, ideas and creations. This is an option for everyone to use. The only access to this is a loving heart that starts with self acceptance and love of self. This is not in a narcissistic way but in a sacred, respectful way.

The yogis and many of the Masters, past and present, know how to slow down their heart beat. They learned how to meditate and to be at one with their whole being, energetically, spiritually, mentally, physically and emotionally. They had a connection to the creator source twenty four seven. This meant that they could 'stand and do' without being in a meditative state if they wished. These tools are available now for you to do the same. This is the age of connection. Indeed, as Kryon teaches us, this is the age of two-way communication with creator source. Isn't that fabulous? This is the power of the 'new human'. The old souls are sensing and realising this first. They have lived the most lifetimes on Mother Earth (at least one hundred and often one thousand) and they are awakening to the truth of who they are. It is beautiful! They are remembering their ancestry and their ancestors. They know, as I do too, that we are our ancestors and that every lifetime builds a library of wisdom, called one's Akash, which is never forgotten by the human being. It is unique to every human and it can be tapped into, to support the human being with their evolutionary growth on the planet in this lifetime.

As an aside even flat worms can remember their past state after they have regenerated themselves with a new head and a new body as appropriate after being cut up! They learn from their previous regeneration. You see we have still to evolve to be able to regenerate our own cell tissues ourselves but all things are possible! Acetabuleria has an amazing genetic make-up as a single-celled algae organism. The genetic control and growth of this 'mermaid's wine glass' plant enables them to do just this – regenerate. It is like a rebirth.

Many 'old souls' are coming together and practising heart coherence. They sit together and focus their energies on those who need support, love and care around the world. The power of one person doing this is good. The power of two people is even more powerful but the power of a large group is totally awesome and is truly felt by those in need. This happened last year with a Kryon group, which was led by Monika Muranyi as the catalyst for such an idea that sent out thought waves with intention of love imagined from Uluru across Australia and infinitely beyond. Within a few days an Australian lady contacted the astrologer, Pam Gregory, and stated that she could feel the love supporting her as they started to assess the damage from the forest wildfires and rebuild their lives.

This is real. Love is real! Kryon explains to us that it will not be long before love is proved. How wonderful will that be for those who only accept scientific proof? Albeit this is kind of odd since love is multi-dimensional and if you cannot feel love then perhaps a little more love of self is needed on one's own journey of self discovery. Ha!

Qi is life force energy and it is up to us to live our best lives possible on Mother Earth. How are you doing?

All of us need a little inspiration and encouragement along the way from time to time and a few tools do not go amiss either so here is a short list of what you can do to support yourself at this most wonderful time:-

1. Drop your karma – decide that only good things are going to come your way!

2. Mix with people who make you laugh and appreciate your own uniqueness and individuality;

3. Make up some affirmations that you feel happy about saying every morning and last thing at night or whenever you want to, to give you a boost and support your focus on what you want to do and how you want to feel;

4. Ask creator source, God, spirit for enhanced intuition;

5. Remember that the free choice of an individual is absolute and so you must ask for everything that you would like;

6. Know that creator source, God, spirit always has your best interests at heart which means that your wishes may not always be fulfilled in your timeframe but they will be fulfilled in divine time!

The simplicity of dropping one's karma really is just that. Karma allowed us the opportunity to learn various lessons from primarily our own past lives' actions as we learned to restore the balance of trust, integrity, love and kindness in this life. That was perfect for the low energy level environment in which most of us were living throughout these times. Since 1989, however, Kryon has been telling us that we no longer need to carry any karma in our energy field because it is no longer serving us. The average energy quotient of this planet has now substantially increased and especially since 21 December 2012, we are as a planet continually moving now into new unchartered territory where we no longer need to hold karmic energy for our highest good.

When we choose a joy-filled, loving state of being the desired focus has now matured to become one of attaining continual balance of the peace that we feel within our loving hearts. And so for those of you who have not yet dropped your karma and/or who are unsure how to do this, may I suggest that you speak the following words to yourself and to your Higher Self/soul (or an equivalent of these words to your liking):-

'I drop my karma and move forward.'

When this or an equivalent word set is spoken with your intention, that is it – done.

Laughter is an amazing tonic for healing one's body at all levels, physically, emotionally, mentally and spiritually. When you are among people whom you respect, like and love then you will feel the energy shift in you and as a group. Do not be surprised if you feel you have more energy around these individuals. When you are having fun working as well as for pleasure, your chakras become more open and balanced which means that you are allowing more natural energy to flow up and down your spinal column. The wonderful aspect of laughter of course is that it is infectious too! Perhaps it is advisable to keep a few tissues handy for those spontaneous tears of joy.

When you redirect your energy from your logical mind to your sensitive and loving heart, you will FEEL the difference in every thought, word and action. Other people will notice this positive change in you. Let your heart guide you from a sense of inner peace. When everything around you seems so surreal and you feel anxious or worried, you can maintain a sense of calmness by going within to soothe all frustration and discontentment.

Allow me to return to the chakra structure and the importance of the energies that are within and around us. Our bodies integrate many invisible energies as these move and shift in the cosmos. Some of you may have had your aura photographed and read by a practitioner to evidence this change over time. Effectively as we evolve and spiritually grow, our chakra system comes into balance as our development impacts on these channels of energy within.

Everything wants to be balanced. Nature wants to be balanced. Human beings want to be balanced. This is the key to being able to flow in life and look upon each day as an adventure of joy-filled love, good health and unlimited abundance.

What will it take to become balanced?

It is important to understand that we are multi-dimensional human beings. There is a whole cellular structure including

approximately 90% of our DNA which is connected to us and presently is often dismissed as existing by the medical profession, even although they assign a name to it termed 'junk DNA'. This is most unfortunate because when one better understands metaphysics and the wholeness of the human being including this approximate eight metre field which is around the physical body of every person then a whole new world of balance becomes more attainable than when this invisible field is ignored. Why? Remember, that everything is connected to everything else. Although you may not yet physically see this field around you, many people can FEEL it as their sensory perceptions are evolving.

I have a great fondness for all things Egyptian and so I will refer to this eight metre field as the Merkaba or Merkabah. In Egyptian, the synthesis of this word embodies three Egyptian words and is explained as follows:-

Mer means light;

Ka means spirit;

Ba means body.

This beautiful invisible field to the naked eye that is around every human is their 'spirit light body'. It is the part of the human being that is the least understood at this time, but once the quantum instrument becomes available (and presently it is under development) with which to see this spectacle, it will change everyone's perspective and perception of how they see themselves and help them to better understand who they are beyond their physical body. We are multi-dimensional beings with an eternal soul.

Furthermore, it is my hope that this invention will be the major catalyst for a paradigm shift in the way that healing and medicine are both taught and practised in future. It is from this 'knowingness' of the magnificence and sacredness of every human being and the integration of their physical body with their spirit light body that has triggered my desire to see built a Centre of Excellence for Healing and Consciousness as the precursor to many such centres around the world.

It is no accident that the heart is the most electro-magnetic organ in the human body, for we are electro-magnetic beings. It is also no surprise that the use of this basic chakra system places the heart at the centre of these seven energy centres.

"

Integrated within your body on this physical planet you are a piece of God that is walking on this earth – at a deep level you know this – there is no God above you – you are a piece of the creator which makes you a magnificent, sacred human being. The God is inside of you. You are the God that is walking on this earth. When you allow yourself to resonate with this truth you begin to understand the power of who you are, the decision choices that you will make and the fact that you have full creative control over your physical life. You are carrying this beautiful energy within you. Your soul is eternal. Time is in a circle. You have lived many lifetimes and will continue to live future lifetimes carrying the soul that is with you on this physical plane. Feel your light that is inside you. Feel and connect with your spirit within you. Your physical body is the vehicle for carrying this light energy. Spirit is always listening to you and supporting you even when you do not make this connection with a part of you.
~ Kryon

Although there are many chakras throughout one's body including in our hands, feet and fingertips, I am going to focus on the seven main chakras as these mirror the seven colours in a rainbow. The word chakra translates literally to mean 'disk' or 'wheel' and the chakra system has its origins in India dating back to over four thousand years. These chakras are essentially pockets of nerve ganglia or energy that reside off the spinal column. They do not exist in the physical sense as they cannot be touched, but they do play a major role in how they impact on our spiritual energy in our Merkaba (our spirit light body). As I mentioned, once the invention of the quantum instrument is available to allow a human being to see the existence of their own Merkaba, this will have a revolutionary effect on how we address our overall health and well-being. For just now, I am asking you to trust this esoteric, metaphysical 'knowingness' that I have (and have used for over fifteen years) to help guide you to balance your own energy body and expand your consciousness as part of your own journey of self-discovery for a fulfilled and healthy long life. Be aware that science is catching up with esoterics!

For ease of understanding imagine that each chakra contains cellular information in the format of a program. When this program becomes corrupted from outside interference of any kind and/or the program becomes outdated and no new upgrade to this program is created for the highest good of the person, then that chakra will become imbalanced.

All seven of these beautiful chakras must be open and spinning at a regular rate to enable the heart, which sits at the centre of these seven chakras, to come into equilibrium with the mind. In this way, both the heart and the mind will be stable and the human being will experience BALANCE.

A chapter has been devoted to each of these seven key chakras. I have chosen to use the appropriate Sanskrit name of these to convey the sacredness and beauty of the role they play in connecting the corporeal body of the human being with their divine essence of consciousness as follows :-

1. Muladhara (governs the coccygeal plexus at the base of the spine)

2. Svadhisthana (governs the hips, genitals, womb, abdomen, lower back areas, all of the skin and the five senses)

3. Manipura (governs the solar plexus)

4. Anahata (governs the heart area)

5. Vissudha (governs the throat)

6. Ajna (governs the third eye which is between the brows)

7. Sahasrara (governs the top of the head cerebral cortex area)

Kryon explains to us that everything has polarity. This includes the human being. It also therefore includes the chakra system. Each of the chakras in the chakra system about which I am writing has polarity which may cause a chakra to become deficient and/or excessive for different reasons. A healthy chakra will have these two polarities restored to balance.

Throughout each chapter I will address the attributes of the specific chakra, identify areas of extreme polarity which may give rise to a deficient and/or excess chakra and explain what may be done to heal and restore balance to this energy centre. In addition, I have suggestions for affirmations to support each 'balanced' chakra.

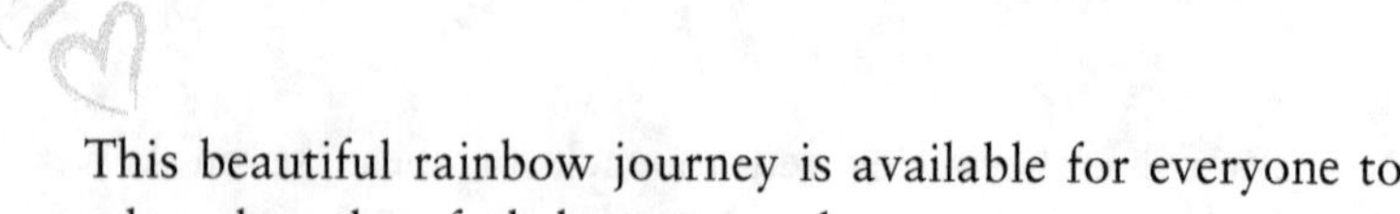

This beautiful rainbow journey is available for everyone to take when they feel they are ready.

Rainbow Alchemy

Let's take a look at the wheels that heal
And connect each person to the universal bridge of colour
With a review of the basic seven chakra systems
Whose patterns interconnect and meld with one another
These centres of activity prefer to be balanced
To receive, assimilate and express life force prana
Which keeps us functioning at optimal levels
Of good health, the first of which is called Muladhara.
At the base of the spine is the red root of survival
An issue geared towards self-preservation
But when we acknowledge the right to have
We are fearless and less dependant on materialism
This grounding in the element Earth
Gives us stability to have physical health
It shapes and forms our physical identity
To manifest abundance including unlimited wealth
The orange sweetness of the second spinning wheel
Governs our sexuality, emotions and sensitivity
Now is the time to manage our feelings
Of self-gratification with great care and fluidity
This chakra's Sanskrit name is Svadhisthana
The element of Water flows with affectionate connection
Our emotional identity forms boundaries of strength
Strong enough to avoid sex addictions and rejection
Manipura is the third wheel of energy encountered
This yellow 'lustrous gem' holds the transformational capacity
Fuelled by the power element of Fire
To be dynamic, spontaneous and full of vitality

Located in the solar plexus it establishes autonomy
Where personal power and responsibility are restored
Self-confidence, reliability and playfulness are present
Over dominance by the ego, however, must not be ignored
To love and be loved is the right of chakra number four
Listen to your heartbeat and the rhythm of its tune
The simplicity of healthy love is experienced in the heart
Reconnect with the air of nature and the Earth Mother's womb
We can heal the green Anahata that often feels in isolation
Rejuvenating the warmth of love that will grow forever true
Creating a unified world of caring, love and compassion
That brings out the divine God and Goddess in you!
There is power in your every thought, action and word
Achieved with the fifth chakra gift of clear communication
How easy is it for you to speak your truth and be heard?
As the turquoise gateway of your throat is boosted by the flow of inspiration
The Vissudha disk of purification opens up our self-expression
You are your own masterpiece of creative innovation
Dispel excessive talking and a fear of aphasia
And focus on good sound quality from this frequency station!
Indigo is the colour of personal insight and illumination
With an ability to hone one's imagination and intuition
The invitation is to go within for what is real
T o experience the third eye of new world vision
The perception of the Ajna shows many dimensions of life
This allows you to transcend the confines of duality
From moment to moment you experience the joy of new birth
And take back control of your own quantum reality!
The seventh wheel of consciousness enhances understanding
With a cool flame of awareness that gives fresh meaning

To the illusion of duality that kept you caged and stagnant
Now setting you free to become a superhuman being!
Unlimited potentials and opportunities are within your reach
The violet Sahasrara is the right to know and learn
You have the ability to think for yourself
It is up to you with your own wisdom, all information to discern
Radiant in love, joy and good health your heart is set free
You've been transformed by the power of your inner light
Filled with grace and balance these chakras align
And forever support you throughout day and night
As spirit and the physical unite in a spiral dance
Congratulations on solving life's mystery through discovery
These healing wheels are inclusive for everyone
Who walks their own soul journey of rainbow alchemy!
~ Lady Wise

CHAPTER 3

Chakra 1
Grounding Your Energy

"

When you connect to your physical reality
You have conquered the aim of the first chakra's strategy
It is a physical communication with our body, Mother Earth
and our surroundings
Best attained when our feet and legs are used
as the key to grounding!
~ Lady Wise

Have you come across health and wellness therapists and consultants mentioning the importance of being grounded? If the answer is yes, perhaps you may have wondered what this means?

Within the context of the chakra system, I consider this to be the most important chakra to be brought into alignment with your body first because it gives you your sense of comfort and security with yourself and the world around you. For simplicity, let's use the analogy of building a house.

A house built on a foundation of sand is not going to last very long at all. Whereas when a house is built with a strong, robust foundation it will have longevity. How we treat our physical body which is on loan to us throughout the time we are on this physical earth is so important not only for our good health and well-being but because without a balanced first chakra a person is unable to manifest.

Kryon explains to us that everything has polarity. This includes the human being. It also therefore includes the chakra system. Each of the chakras in the chakra system about which I am writing has polarity which may cause a chakra to become deficient and/or excessive for different reasons. A healthy chakra will have these two polarities restored to balance.

What is the importance of the first chakra in this seven chakra system to our energy body embracing our spiritual, emotional, mental and physical needs?

When a baby is born by a natural birth then the crown chakra will be the first chakra to have the spiritual life force pressed into it as the child comes down the birth canal and is birthed head first into the world followed by the spiritual enlivening of all the other six chakras. The quality of this prana, chi or energy which enters the physical body is dependant on so many different factors. For example, if a child is born in a warm, quiet, relaxed environment and immediately post birth the mother shows great love and joy at receiving the baby in her arms without complications, then the likelihood is that a strong bonding will form between them which will only strengthen in their lifetime and furthermore the connection of spirit with the physical body will be appropriately anchored and the child will grow up feeling safe and secure. On the other hand, if a baby is born under extreme conditions affecting its environment and/or experiences complications arising at birth then these may affect the root chakra at the base of the spine denoting survival. Impairment of the initial developmental stage of that baby may remain with that person into their adolescent and adult life if the original program in that first chakra is never changed.

Remember that our energy bodies are made up of many patterns or programs that we can choose to change. When we continue to live our life on old programs and old patterning then we can become stuck in our lives and never understand why. All we need to do is adjust a few things within our energy bodies to allow the space to bring in new programs that will start to serve us for the dynamic life that we want.

The foundation of our survival is the right to be here and to exist. This Muladhara or root chakra covers the stage in the womb up to twelve months old. The confidence of a child's right to be here will include how the mother has cared for her baby in the womb since conception up to child birth and beyond. When a child is born out of less desirable circumstances and is not wanted, this patterning will be imprinted on the blueprint of that child's first chakra. If a mother has spent much of her time in front of a television and used her mobile phone regularly throughout her pregnancy then the frequency waves and resonance of her baby's first chakra will be adversely affected more than if she had spent her time in nature and talking to her child in the womb, perhaps singing to it throughout her pregnancy, before it was born.

It is important that a baby is born into the world with as healthy a first chakra as possible. This implies that the mother takes responsibility for the prenatal development stage of its life as well as once it has been physically born. The child that is felt loved and welcomed into the world will express different personality traits than one who has been neglected and denied its basic rights of care. How we show up in later life in terms of our confidence, our health, our ability to make good decisions, feeling assured about our financial prosperity and abundance, all originates from this first chakra. It is the foundation of our life and it is imperative that we have this strong and healthy connection with our body. The formation of the physical identity of the child in the early months as well as the building up and strengthening of its physical body will be greatly determined by how a parent approaches this survival care. Once born, a baby is totally reliant on care to have all of its needs met. If any of these needs are denied or delayed then similarly this may have a negative impact on that child's first chakra in its older years too. For example, when a baby cries and that cry is for food but the food is denied the child for some time, then this builds in a fear to the first chakra because a basic need is not being met. This fear can be initiated across every attribute of its life from the response to a baby's cry when it wakes up from sleep, how quickly its nappy is responsibly changed, how soon it is lifted up and held once it has started to cry. It does not get any more basic than satisfying the baby's need for food, shelter, warmth and the human touch because the baby has zero independence at this time. It's nurture and nourishment rests entirely with its parents.

When a child is born it has no understanding of the separation of itself from its surroundings. Everything is effectively all merged into a 'oneness' (which as an adult we can take years to come back to with understanding and maturity of the chakra system cycle). This explains why the beauty, comfort and security of its surroundings are so important as well as the love, care and focus given on the child in its early stages. All of these aspects are contributing to the creation of its personality.

Throughout the prenatal and first twelve months of its life, the baby's main focus is on that of its mother and on its internal world of consciousness. Only once the child starts to sit, walk, reach for things and perhaps crawl, does it then begin to understand that it is separate from its mother. I mentioned perhaps crawl because apparently I chose not to crawl and just decided to stand up and walk one day. Ha! You see we are each so very different and unique. There is no right or wrong way.

One of the most important factors I want to convey about this first chakra to amazing pregnant ladies and to those who have recently given birth is never to underestimate the importance of every thought, word and action about your child. This beautiful baby may not yet be able to walk, talk and respond to you in its early months of living but it is absorbing every energetic wave of experience with you. Do you realise that some parents' fears may be inherited by the child? There is so much core truth in maintaining a healthy, positive outlook on life and yet so few people choose to live by this and some even ridicule those who live by this mantra because they themselves are so much in denial of their own spirit and body connection that they cannot observe their own dysfunctionality and removal from the daily aliveness and joy of living which is their birthright!

We each need a strong foundation of 'home' within our physical body from which to anchor in spirit and the other chakras as we go on this soul journey of the rainbow bridge to wholeness uniting mind and body, the divine masculine with the divine feminine, and connecting the beautiful divine spark of consciousness that is within us to the consciousness of the external world of creation.

This rooting into the earth of our first chakra gives us structure and boundaries from which we experience life and feel secure and supported in all we do. Any weaknesses, energy leakages or tears in this first chakra which go unidentified may give rise in later years to key issues affecting our health, prosperity and job prospects as examples.

Nature itself is such a great teacher for us. This grounding into the earth of our being is no different to a seed that is planted which grows and reaches for the skies, thriving well with a firm root base. Beech trees, for example, do not have deep roots compared to oak trees. This means that with very heavy rain over time their roots may become so saturated with water that they are uprooted with the next gale force winds to arrive. The strong, sturdy oak trees, however, which have their roots more deeply embedded in the earth will generally stand for longer under similar weather conditions regardless of how tall they are. The strength of a person's natural instincts to survive and their confidence of their right to be here and to have, as an illustration, good food, good health, a great family, a lovely home and a job that they love doing, are dependant on an harmonious balanced first chakra.

Perhaps you have heard of the expression 'They'll be ok, they can stand on their own two feet'. This expression implies that the person can look after themselves and has what is needed to survive. In reality, it is so much more than this. A balanced first chakra oriented to self-preservation and an individual who feels that they have a strong connection with their biological body and are confident of their body as a 'sacred temple' is vital as the catalyst for the journey up through the other six chakras and back down these channels of energy to the first chakra in order to manifest.

Allow me to use the metaphor of a motor car and car key or Smartphone app used to open and close the car doors to illustrate the importance of the first chakra in your body. If you forget your key, bring the wrong key, forget your Smartphone or do not have it charged or have it accidentally stolen, then you are denied swift access to your vehicle. It matters not that your beautiful car is clean and polished with the latest music equipment and surround sound, gadgetry, sports seats and seven speed gear box. If you cannot access it with ease then you are denied the enjoyment of all these other attributes. Having your car's physical key or Smartphone app predicates you being able to take those marvellous car journeys and experience fun in your vehicle. It is the primordial tool for motoring. Equally, a strong and balanced first chakra in your body is the mainstay for everything else that happens in your life.

The areas of the body that are associated with the first chakra are the feet, legs and the base of the spine known also as the coccygeal plexus. Our feet are the ground for our body, for our roots. This chakra corresponds to the element of earth and this should alert us to the core truth that we are allied with nature. Sadly, this alliance is seldom taught to children at this time and has been 'missed' out of religious practices and doctrines. Once again if one researches the indigenous tribes from around the world, all of them honour,

respect and ally with nature for their survival and prosperity, taking from the earth only what they need. They are connected with their environment and respect it as much as they do their physical bodies. They take time to listen to their ancestors and to glean the knowledge of the earth. They know that for every disease (dis-ease) there is a plant antidote. This is the essence of how nature works.

A short exercise to help you ground your energy is as follows:-

Take a moment to stand or sit still and be comfortable and relaxed. The important thing is to relax. Have your body relaxed whether you are standing or sitting. The outcome of this exercise is best felt when you have bare feet and are standing on grass, sand or soil but this is not mandatory. During this exercise it is preferably to have your eyes gently closed. Find a position of comfort and place your feet flat on the ground. Be aware of your breathing but do not over breathe. Imagine that you are breathing out all the stress, fear, worry and anxiety and breathing in fresh, beautiful, uplifting, nourishing energy. Allow your breathing to stay calm. Feel safe and secure. As you are completely relaxed bring your attention to your feet and imagine strong, healthy roots, akin to tree roots, growing out of the soles of your feet and expanding downwards and outward into the fertile soil of Mother Earth, spreading out across a vast area as you effectively 'root yourself' in your mind into the existence of the magnificent person that you are on this physical plane. If you feel uncomfortable at any time you can just open your eyes. Now simultaneously feel the increasing surge of energy rise up into your feet connecting you with Gaia and embracing your physical body. Feel the downward/outward energy anchor you into the earth as you exhale and as you take a breath in, feel the inward energy rise up from the soles of your feet into your legs as if this energy is pulling you back to gravity like a suction pump sealing in the nourishment you need for your existence on Pachamama. I suggest doing this for about eleven minutes. Gently open your eyes and take a moment to adjust and bring yourself into full waking consciousness feeling fully grounded in your body and feeling wonderful.

When any chakra is out of balance and alignment and in this particular case, when the first chakra is out of balance the reason may be due to:-

- a deficiency;

- an excess in that chakra or

- a combination of both a deficiency reason and an excess reason.

We are only given one body in a lifetime and so without connecting with it and without honouring it as our temple of opportunity and our tool to help us to thrive and feel fully alive, the first chakra will become imbalanced and dysfunctional. Unless a human being is able to express their feelings and emotions in an honest, straightforward way that is understood by others then physical ailments will manifest in the human body. And so for someone to be feeling vulnerable, afraid, mistrusting of others and filled with a lack of self-confidence and self-esteem, that person will struggle in their ability to connect with the outside world and their environment.

This particular chakra is the foundation of our existence, of our 'home' while we are alive on the earth plane and its

initial formation goes back to the prenatal stage. What does this mean? It means that how a mother has reacted throughout her pregnancy will also majorly contribute to the development of this first chakra in the baby.

If the mother was prone to taking alcohol, drugs and/or smoked then this 'feeds the unborn child' too since the foetus is part of the mother. There is no exclusion boundary around the unborn child to prevent it from receiving the food taken and experiences absorbed by its mother. Similarly, if the mother suffered from hypertension, anxiety and felt insecure for example, then this would be felt by the unborn baby in the form of a contracted womb that was tight, when the mother felt mistrusting of her environment and/or the people around her during pregnancy. An unborn baby has no power to control the flow of energy into their developing little body therefore they are unable to prevent unwanted energy into their system.

Basically everything that the mother experiences during pregnancy the unborn baby shares in these times too to the extent that it significantly shapes the condition of the child's first chakra once it is born and is a contributing factor to the trust and security that the baby feels even before it has lived out its first twelve months.

This begins to give you an idea of how deeply connected we are to our mothers in utero because we are so closely bonded throughout this time prior to being birthed into this current life to the extent that all memories are stored. Many people have accurately remembered their experiences during this prenatal period and later had these confirmed by their parents. Sometimes it's emotions, feelings or even physical sensations including those of one's mother or father, because consciousness is not limited to the physical body and so one can pick up those physical sensations, emotions or impressions of either parent.

What we need to remember is that absolutely everything that happens both in utero and to the baby once it is born forms memories that that little person never forgets. They are all lodged in the Akash even when in adult years the grown up infant cannot consciously remember them. When an individual has endured traumatic experiences they may have consciously blocked these memories out to the extent that potentially important mental and emotional states go unreleased.

In severe instances, physical ailments may manifest as a result of not addressing these mental and emotional issues and that person will struggle to move forward in their life. One method that can ease the blockage of forgotten memories and pinpoint where symptoms first began is to undertake a past life regression. Pain phobias and fears work well with this healing strategy because when the person recognises that a symptom commenced in a past life and not in the present, very often the symptom starts to disappear as they accept and release the memory.

Dr. Brian Weiss whom I met several years ago is my favourite mentor in this field and I would recommend his books and/ or a workshop as an introductory taster to this healing discipline. In his first book on this subject, "Many Lives, Many Masters" he writes beautifully about his encounter with a client who regressed more than four thousand years when asked under regression therapy when her first symptoms began. This was a surprise to both of them at that time because neither of them believed in past lives! Indeed, back in 1980 because Brian had been formally trained in chemistry

and as a scientist, he was very left-brained about the whole thing and sceptical. Now there are hundreds of thousands of collective stories about past lives.

We really do not know what we do not know and I would suggest that in this new paradigm of shift worldwide, with every step that you take allow yourself to be self-aware and open to grow in knowledge and wisdom. Expect the unexpected! When you keep an open mind you are open to learning new things.

I can recollect very clearly sitting alongside my Mum's hospital bed and awkwardly supporting her on and off for about five hours while she spoke in a completely different language to another energy force in the room. It was remarkable and I feel very privileged and honoured to have experienced this. Although I love learning languages and used to be fluent in three other European languages many years ago, like most things unless the practice is put in we become a little rusty. The words that my Mum spoke, however, were not of a modern language. To this day I do not yet know which language she was speaking. Intuitively I felt it may have been Hebrew. It was coming through her Higher Self and at times she was rather annoyed and was quick to retort to the energy present. Although I could not translate the numerous words spoken by her I instinctively felt as if she was negotiating to stay longer with me on Mother Earth before she passed. As soon as a nurse entered to check and turn her on the bed she would revert to her conscious 'unconscious state' unable to speak or open her eyes. It really was most remarkable and somehow I am expecting to receive an explanation for this in this lifetime to help me grow in my own knowledge. There is so much about the mind and our Higher Self that we have still to learn and understand.

It's so exciting because through this knowledge we will be able to help protect vulnerable human beings and guide them to personal solutions and a more balanced life.

A deficiency in a person's Muladhara indicates that they are unable to build up sufficient energy in this chakra to reach a balanced point. They need to find ways of charging up their channels of energy to increase the 'size of their vessel' in order to hold the necessary energy to be able to create and manifest what they desire. Whatever they have been doing they are unable to retain the energy produced. There may be a disconnect in accepting who they are and in expressing their emotions which build up inner tension and stress, ultimately manifesting fears and a lack of harmony in their life.

Examples of a deficient first chakra are often very visible from the physical structure and outline of an individual's body. Imagine someone who is so unhappy when they wake up in the morning that they seriously feel that they do not want to be here on Mother Earth. How do you think this extreme sadness will affect their body shape? Do you think that the overall size and scale of their body would be proportionate to their desire to be alive? Over long periods of time, it would be usual to observe a person who is very thin and may have severe health problems such as eating disorders, digestive disorders and/or a whole host of issues with their feet, legs, knees and/or posterior. Such disconnection and disillusionment with life may also extend to physical health challenges affecting the bones and teeth as these body parts also fall under this first chakra location. Bones and teeth are part of our physical structure which creates our basic form at birth. These issues are expressed in this physical form because an individual feels a disconnect with the ease

and grace of living their dreams on the physical plane. They are so removed from feeling joy and love/being loved in their life that they want to escape from living. Any contact in the physical world may be really difficult for them and they may feel that they simply want to hide away from everyone and not be seen. They are likely to be dominated by the thoughts in their mind which are preventing them from experiencing a whole mind and body harmony that would otherwise enable them/ support them in fulfilling their wishes and desires in life.

Given that a person's physical body is their 'vessel' and structure for supporting them at a basic needs level, I hope you can empathise with how a considerably underweight person may view their world and feel very afraid and insecure. Such anxieties and restlessness from an inability to manifest even the most basic of needs such as enough money to pay bills, purchase food and other household essentials impact that person's ability to concentrate, hold down a job and satisfactorily manage their finances, as just a few examples. They can often be very troubled with their emotions which will carry into their work environment and may show up as an inability to focus on the task required. Furthermore, they are likely to be extremely disorganised and feel a great restlessness within themselves that means they are unproductive at whatever they do and have trouble completing work. Such a lack of discipline, determination and focus may mean that it is not long before that person finds themselves out of a job and 'hopping' from one job to another in order to make ends meet. Such frustration may add to that individual experiencing dark thoughts and feeling totally incapable of moving forward in their life with light in their heart and immeasurable joy. Moreover, they may have issues with living beyond their means which gives rise to financial difficulties. All in all they are likely to be unstable because there is no structure to their body and to their life in terms of being able to confidently move forward with clarity of mind and an ability to focus on achieving their desires. They may feel there is no hope for the future and have deep relationship problems with other people expecting them to provide the support and guidance that is needed all the time rather than taking responsibility for their own actions. Such low level consciousness and being tied up in one's mind all the time does not allow for that person to breakthrough and discover their own inner power that is more than capable of carrying them through life in joy, love and harmony which is the sustenance and glorious support for their own chakra journey of the soul.

When the container that is the body and framework for all of life's experiences appears so thin, there is no room for that person to hold good health and vitality. It is as if one has a watering can with holes in the bottom of it. The watering can would no longer be able to contain water without extensive repair work being done.

The good news is, as with all the seven chakras, that there are healing options available to help balance the chakra. Indeed, increasingly more and more healing modalities are being introduced to us to help the healing journey. In addition to various physical, emotional, spiritual and mental help that is available, affirmations are also a wonderful support tool to assist in recalibrating and restoring a chakra to harmony and balance.

Our body is integral to who we are and to the connection that we have with our mind and with spirit. When a human

being is in denial about the condition of their body and treats it and speaks about it as if it was an object and something that is separate to them then there will be disharmony in the first chakra.

It may be that there is a tear in the chakra or perhaps an energy leakage, in which case the person will not feel their sense of security restored until this chakra is healed. This, incidentally, may relate to other chakras in one's body too.

We must learn to unconditionally love our body and to combat our fears about scarcity, safety, trust and security for a healthy first chakra as we live with our sacred temple in the physical world, recognising it as the engine to our whole system of energy. Listen to the messages of your body where you have experienced illness or pain.

So much of the trauma associated with an imbalanced first chakra originates from that person's childhood experiences. It takes effort, time and respect for one's healing journey to deconstruct the embedded patterns and programs from that time to then assimilate, determine and reconstruct the appropriate healing practices to correct this. In this lifetime right now much of the imbalance showing up in a person's physical body is due to an accumulation of unhealed trauma across lifetimes and not necessarily specific to this lifetime. Anything rooted in a deeper level of fear is synonymous with the first chakra. The unravelling of a person's root chakra experiences requires to be recognised and understood for that person to receive the healing they need and to allow them to then respect the past and create the new programs sufficient for a healthy Muladhara that will function perfectly as the foundation platform of the other six chakras.

The survival instincts of a healthy root channel of energy should be instinctive so that they 'kick in' to action under extreme emergency situations rather than being stuck in a continuous 'panic mode' because of childhood troubles that have gone unresolved at a mental and emotional level. This is simply an old energy program that requires to be identified, brought to the surface and then healed to enable a new program to be introduced that will allow the human being to be centred and balanced in this first chakra.

An excess in a person's Muladhara indicates that they are unable to discharge the energy that they have built up in this chakra. They have too much energy in this energy channel and it becomes stuck with no place to move. In a healthy first chakra the energy produced would naturally move upwards and propel the energy into activating the second and other upward chakras. In an excess scenario this is not happening yet similarly the individual is unable to send the energy downwards into the earth to make them feel more grounded. They become stuck and feel unable to move forward in their daily life. Until they make a change this discombobulated chakra pattern will repeat and repeat.

Old patterns of action that are no longer serving us need to be brought up, recognised, almost 'digested' as a turn of expression and then released. When a person lets go these patterns of behaviour it allows space for expansion, taking things in a lighter mood with laughter and experiencing an enhanced wisdom rather than holding on to a fear that is no longer in alignment with your greater sense of being.

Some reasons of excess experienced in the first chakra may be as follows:-

In the same way that a deficient chakra was characterised with weight loss, an excessive chakra may be identified from a person who is carrying a large amount of weight beyond their suggested average weight for their height. In addition, they may have a tendency to overeat. Such obesity and/or craving to eat may be rooted in a person's fear from when they were young that there was never enough food to eat. When food is presented to the person in adulthood they may continue to eat without having the program set within, almost like a boundary, to cease eating once thorough and sufficient nourishment has been enjoyed. Instead, the program that runs inside the human being alerts fearful limitless scoffing as if the next meal is not guaranteed.

I have noticed a similar survival approach taken by animals which have been starved of regular food especially with cats and dogs. The survival tendency is that when food does appear a hungry animal may eat and eat far more than their stomach is capable of digesting. This action then prompts digestive health challenges because the stomach has shrunk due to a lack food previously made available to it and is now being pumped with too much food because the animal which has had the food presented to it, senses it should simply eat and eat until all the food is gone regardless of how much is adequate for its metabolism. All fear that exists within an animal or a person creates a cycle of unhealthy patterns.

Someone who is unable to discharge the build up of energy on their first chakra may also be perceived by others as lazy, a bit dull and lacking in drive to do things. They may express a lack of curiosity in a willingness to listen to something new, and ability to seek out new interests and adventures. Very often this negative aspect manifests itself in extreme tiredness and a general reluctance to do only the most essential and basic of tasks to get by. Furthermore, another attribute of this excess is an unwillingness to change anything.

The essence of becoming balanced is to be the change that you want to be. Wonderful new possibilities and potentials are emerging in this new energy since 2012 to help individuals to make a change and to make it easier for them to do this first, at an energetic level. The degree of difficulty in altering old habits to become a person with a more positive, upbeat, harmonious state of being rests entirely with aligning with what feels good at all levels. When an individual has never been used to setting any boundaries in their life for living from a survival perspective (and not from an enlightened, higher thinking perspective covered under chakra seven when to have unlimited boundaries of the imagination is to become free to expand one's mind for unlimited potential) then decision-making at this root level becomes almost non-existent. A person's mind will be very fickle and constantly jump around as they feel unable to feel secure and protected in daily life.

In a similar way, an excess chakra may reveal itself through a person obsessed with material gain. In extreme cases this can result in hoarding. Sadly I have seen how this can not only completely restrict a person from feeling alive but it can physically restrict them from being able to freely move around their home and also drive in their car, when both are stacked to the ceiling and roof respectively with stuff. This is a tangible display of a person's first chakra insecurity and lack of trust in a universe that can abundantly provide for everyone, not just them, without limitation.

It is really important not to become enslaved to our mind. Our mind is not our master. We are the Master of our mind when we attain a fully vital seven chakra system that is in balance and harmony with our body, mind and the environment. This mastery shows up in the immanence which lights up our whole face and especially shows in the sparkle of our eyes and our aura.

Without balance in this first chakra we are unable to activate the imagination and creativity which is the reason we are here as awesome creators! Are you remembering that when we reconnect with that divine spark that is within each one of us and raise our vibration we are also enabled to reconnect with our wonderful entourage? This is the energy support of our spirit guides and ancestors who have the ancient wisdom at our disposal! All we need to do is call it in.

We are never alone and it is imperative that I reiterate this so that you realise that all your responsibilities may be shared with your Higher Self and your entourage to guide you for your highest good. The difference in this new energy is that you have the power from within you to take control over your life without looking for constant outside help. As an empowered individual you will feel strong and confident in your uniqueness no matter what you do. Your creativity will begin to overflow with ideas and as a genuinely joyful person others will want to be around you simply for the positive vibe that you exude. A person who is balanced feels power-full instead of power-less. You will feel liberated from being 'more of you' in your magnificence and feel safe and secure in your decision-making as well as physically.

There are no definitive guidelines for healing the wounds (mental, emotional and physical) of the first chakra that may have been embedded as far back as the initial developmental stages of childhood. Rather, it is appropriate that each person is treated as the unique breathing magnificent specimen of humanity that they are in all their beauty with respect and dignity. Without the specifics of a one-to-one client appointment, however, I will offer general guidance on healing for an imbalanced first chakra.

The basic foundation of the physical body is that it is built to survive. It would be normal to expect that a person can live without continually being in fear of their life, for example. Unless we can establish a healthy first chakra, our attention will be directed away from all the other chakras with an obsessive and unhealthy focus on this first chakra. It is not uncommon to identify the reason for imbalance having been triggered by fear. Dark and light, fear and love are two of the best known attributes of the duality in which most people are living presently. When you understand what is happening then you are in a better informed position to make the best choices for yourself.

Trust that you are love. Love and fear cannot co-exist. We are in a paradigm shift presently. Shift is happening all the time on this planet. It means that when you shift your thinking then everything around you shifts too!

Consciousness is energy. This has been proved. In this new energy more 'Old Souls' (who have experienced at least one hundred lifetimes on planet earth to date and often as many as one thousand) are willing to see more and are aware that things are changing to the extent that humanity is becoming kinder and more compassionate. As a planet, this civilisation is evolving. Remember as a human race we generally loathe the prospect of change yet without it we never grow emotionally, mentally and spiritually!

Dark and light are metaphors for different kinds of consciousness that humans develop. It is not about demons or other entities. It is about human beings. Kryon's teachings inform us about preparing for the balance between light and dark. The balance between low and high consciousness on this planet has always generally been skewed in a way that is dark.

I tend to think of low consciousness as low level thinking and higher consciousness as higher level thinking. To this extent I consider that low level thinking is indicative of a human being who is trapped by their own mindset into thinking that they are separate from the connection to any other human being and are only interested in their own self gain at the expense of another, void of self-respect, respect for anyone else, grasping at life in all its forms and convinced that the world is full of limitations – limited money, limited food, limited love and limited resources.

On the other hand, a person of higher level thinking has a balanced set of seven chakras and has an inner 'knowingness' that they are connected to everything (not just all other human beings) by the spark of divinity that is inside them and with which all human beings have been born. They have no fear and instead are strongly grounded in their own energy. Furthermore, they are alert, vital and always aware of their surroundings consciously choosing those environments where they feel comfortable and where they can enjoy downtime with other 'kindred spirits' and like-minded thinkers who possess a healthy heart expressing kindness, love and compassion. They are assertive, confident and know who they are. Among their fellow 'tribe' it would not be perceived as unusual to sing and dance regularly in celebration of the joy of life!

Since 2012 there has been an increase in the light quotient in consciousness which is beginning to develop all around the globe more than at any other time in history. What does this mean? The result is that we are starting to see more of the darkness, ugliness and horror of how humans have treated and do still treat other humans.

The balance between the light and the dark energies (the metaphor for consciousness) is beginning to change. It is becoming more balanced with an increase in light. Indeed, for the last eight years there has been a tipping point in favour of the light energies between low and high consciousness. Have you noticed this in the social media news? When natural disasters happen across the world, for example, the general response to such 'dark' events is an outpouring of greater kindness and compassion. Even with a little light shift, we are also beginning to see the reporting of the darkest things such as human trafficking issues. Dark energy that comes from consciousness which is low, creates systems that do not work, dysfunctional belief systems and creates many dark things that are only a reflection of themselves.

The acceleration of these Changeover Years is now moving at a faster pace than it has ever done over the last seven to eight years. There is no need to be afraid because these times are different. There is nothing in history against which to compare this. The future measured in decades is going to be wonderful. There will be no competition of resources. A dysfunctional dark mind will decide in advance of what is coming and it will not be pleasant and focus on perceived 'doom and gloom'! On the other hand, there will be those people who resonate with the increased light on this planet and who can see and trust that the inappropriateness will be cleared up.

*Light is shining and being shown in dark places and
across the world we are seeing what has been happening.*
~ Kryon

We are having our eyes wide opened with an increased awareness that is part of humanity maturing. Now that your consciousness is starting to include more light your awareness to these issues is heightened. The wonderful outcome to this is that we will find solutions to help and prevent such dark events and scenarios from continuing in the future.

It is so important at this time to be able to stay well, stay healthy and to build up your immune system so that you are energised for imagining new pathways of creative expression, dreams and desires that are bigger for you than on any previous scale. The sadness and horror of the dark events and happenings that are being brought to the surface by the increased light and made known world-wide are uncovering what has been around for hundreds of years and been previously hidden.

Can you relax knowing that you are seeing these human stories being told and truth revealed? Know in your heart that there are those people who will find new ways of preventing such heinous activities from happening in the future and to this extent the uncovered tragedies have been revealed to allow much healing to occur. This healing extends beyond those individuals who have sadly lost their lives to the darkness. This healing extends beyond those victims of the darkness who remain alive with medical conditions as a result of their abuses and traumas. This is healing on a global scale and it starts with those persons who feel that the darkness uncovered has been disturbing at a conscious level.

Kindness, love and compassion are slowly replacing the dark energy around the planet.

Light is world wide. It is for everyone. Wake up! The darkness of confusion, delusion, dictatorship, illusion and inappropriateness is starting to be seen all across the globe.

We need to see the dark aspects both within ourselves and around us in the external world in order to clean them up with new innovations, systems, processes and new solutions as we begin to think differently with the help of our intuition!

When we can open up to a new orientation about ourselves first, question and find the truth about what we value in life now, then we can reclaim our own true values and take control of our lives, regardless of what is going on in the outside world. We can stand strong in who we are and what type of life we want to create for ourselves from a strong first chakra. We feel deserving of being alive. We feel worthy of being alive. It is your birthright to be here. It is ok if you have forgotten this. There are many light workers here to support you on your soul journey of self-transformation. You have beautiful, uplifting, loving memories of how you have been loved in this life and past lives. Any forgetfulness of these is coming back. The overall low consciousness of Mother earth for eons has prevented so many from remembering all the good memories and has tended to focus on only the dark dreams.

At a scientific level, however, there is polarity in everything. Our Akashic memories are going to start to change and we will start to have visions and dreams of joy. This is the reflection of a polarity that is starting to change. Consciousness starts to repair itself and become a little more elegant. Our Akash is reflecting back to us the polarity that is changing

with the dark/light relationship as we are beginning to have more light, metaphorically.

Hip, hip, hurrah for the increasing balance of consciousness on the planet! This brings with it a mix of light and dark dreams, instead of only dark dreams.

Personally, I want to be able to remember and revisit things from the past which are real that are of lightness, joy and love.

Too many of us have been and are consumed with reflecting on memories that are dark. There is no need for you to remember the sadness and stories of horror anymore. We have created a consciousness that reflects the weakest part, the darkest things of our past. You are not defined by what has happened in your past. It is not who you are. You are a magnificent human being with a Higher Self who has been caught up in an old program running with the weak force. You have polarity. That means you can change the way you think if you want to. That means when you work with yourself you can reflect on all these dark, heartfelt issues, you can shift and see the light part, the stronger part as opposed to the weak element which is the darker part. When we work with the light aspect we come to understand and feel the knowingness and the assurance that our loved-ones lost are still with us. They have a divine spark inside, an eternal soul, which means that when they die they transmute into another energy form.

In reality, a piece of their soul becomes embedded in your (multi-dimensional) soul and they are with you until the day you die. The light will start to help balance you up. The world has this strong (light) and weak (dark) force for every single atom.

Can you see the light from all those stories that happened to you at the time it was needed and see the love that was needed to kick you into touch for where you are now? This is the light of a situation that supports you and keeps you from waking up at night with only a weak perspective. If you can allow for this shift by relaxing into your daily life and to the natural flow of everything you do without the need to logically control every aspect, then you will start to bring back your own balance by living out whatever feels good for you and all that is for your highest good. Free choice is absolute. You no longer need to be controlled by the dark. This is the hope of an evolving consciousness and a human being who knows that there is more even when you do not know exactly what this is or understand it.

The analogy that I would use for myself is that of a computer. I do not need to understand HOW the computer works as long as I have access to all the software programs that I need. Things are not always as they seem. Your loved ones lost are still with you until your last breath. Knowing this core truth gave me so much comfort when my Mum died and it also meant that with this 'bird's eye view' and higher perspective of knowing what the birth, death, birth, death cycle was all about, I was able to find an inner strength to plan her funeral as a celebration of life rather than focusing on the sadness of how I felt in having to now live without her physical presence. Thankfully, we were always very close (presumably from a close bond formed in the womb and both being 'Old Souls' experiencing many past lives together). While she was alive I would often describe my adventures abroad to her and she would listen intently imagining for herself what joys and laughter I had encountered. Now that both Dad and Mum have passed, they are able to come with me 24/7! Ha! They share in the experience and I never have to explain anything! I am also able to call them in and ask for their guidance whenever it suits me.

This is only a small part of how our own insight (from looking more closely within ourselves) is able to aid our own spiritual development and soul journey growth. This is a form of natural healing that is available to everyone who can let go old patterns of fear and insecurity to make space for reforming, remoulding and creating new streamlined programs to meet our evolutionary needs in 2020 and beyond.

Light is starting to win…slowly!

In the past, there has been a tendency to feel that in order to move forward in our life we have had to have outside help from others to do this. In using and believing in this approach we have then given away our power by allowing other people to make up our minds for us because we have not started from a grounding point of stability and security. This is an old paradigm and is no longer appropriate now that we are existing in new energy since December 2012.

As an alternative, there is now an opportunity to seek the appropriate guidance from a teacher who can explain to you how to empower yourself to be able to go within and decide on the best choices for you as you learn to open up your perspective on life from a higher vantage point. Think about the beauty and majesty of an eagle soaring over the countryside able to see clearly what the possibilities are for it. This powerful bird has strong vision and the space to choose numerous options of how to carefully land a mouse, for example. From the perspective of the mouse on the ground, however, its view is very shady and restricted from the long grasses in its path. It is living with greater uncertainty about what is ahead of it by only a few paces because it is surviving from a lower perspective than the eagle and does not have clarity of its location.

It is totally different to have a strong sense of self and ask other people for information so that you can gather the data, collate the different perspectives and viewpoints and then make your own balanced decisions from this exercise. When it comes to the first chakra, however, the basic mindset of an imbalanced chakra is instability, insecurity and an inability to make decisions. There may be a temptation to make a quick decision that is not based on all the relevant facts, simply because the mind cannot hold focus and attention for very long. Under these circumstances initial help from others is needed until you have worked through the issue of being able to balance your first chakra and maintain this harmony in your life.

The necessary help and guidance that you need will enable and empower you to learn how to make decisions on your own but only from a centred place of balance and harmony. As hundreds of thousands more humans start to awaken they will remember their own unique gifts and want to serve others in turn with their growth by becoming teachers and guides on this.

Historically, these people would be considered outsiders to the rest of their community because they appear different. Those who have this aptitude can stand on their own feet and have gone within themselves to connect to the Higher Self inside which is a multi-dimensional source. At this level of consciousness it comes with an entourage that is known by the human being with elevated inner awareness. These

human beings are allowed to connect with their entourage because although they do not understand everything that exists in this multi-dimensionality they trust that it is for their highest good and are content to simply 'be' with this limited knowledge until such time as they are informed of the bigger picture.

Did you know that you are born magnificent and you die magnificent? Since 2012, new benevolent and loving energy has been pouring into planet Earth through twelve pairs of nodes and nulls around the world. It was all timed by our esoteric parents the Pleiadians if we ever reached the marker point of 21 December 2012, which humanity did. Wow!

This 'Shift' on Mother Earth is the beginning of a new paradigm for us all. Our souls, and in particular 'Old Souls', have never experienced this before on this planet. What is remarkable, however, is that our eternal soul knows what to do with this change and how to intuitively guide us through the process, which is why it is important that we do not allow our mind to overrule our intuition. This is a time when our divine feminine and divine masculine energies are working harmoniously together to help us each become our own integrated, balanced, whole soul person. Once we are able to get into our physical body and relate to it as part of our wholeness of being, then we can learn to calm it down and realise that there is nothing that we cannot achieve when we have intention, clarity of mind and motivation.

You are magnificent!

Beautiful helpers of the creator made with purity and light
Appear when you need them throughout day and night
They come in with your energy when you are first birthed
And forever stay with you until your last breath on earth
All you need to remember is that you are never alone
You can communicate with them using your
internal phone
There is no telephone number to be memorised
For they are already part of your being inside
Now is the time to learn and connect
Through the power of your heart – out of love
and respect
Once you overcome the pitfalls of darkness
You become able to elevate your awareness
And earn access to your own entourage of transformation
From which you can manifest your dreams with
successful activation
This is how God works with the creation of the
human being
Which relies on your ability to trust without seeing!
The angels are a metaphor for your magnificence and for
your spiritual intuition
Representing a consciousness of light which you spark
with your decision
Imagine your heart as the sun and your mind as
the clouds
Be forever reminded that there are no pockets in a shroud
For as long as the cloud is of a darker consciousness the
angels are denied access by YOU!
Perhaps it is time for you to awaken to a higher
spiritual truth.

It is one of the most difficult things to explain a sample of what exists in a multi-dimensional reality to a person who has not yet experienced a taste of their own multi-dimensionality and remains in a linear reality. Often the confusion and curiosity in a person starts when they become aware that there are more realities than the one reality – their current reality – which exist.

As you start clearing the cloud, metaphorically speaking, with your higher thinking, your own magnificence starts to shine through and you are allowed to receive the benevolent energies in to work with you in raising your consciousness.

You are already magnificent!

So what can be done to heal and restore balance to this first chakra?

Fear that is lodged in the first chakra needs to be moved through the physical movement in one's body. Any kind of physical exercise would therefore be encouraged especially walking, running, jumping up and down, hopping, skipping and dancing. It is very easy to purchase weights and to use these in your own home without the need for further expense in joining a local gym or sports club that you may seldom frequent. Even small supermarkets are selling yoga mats these days and so you may decide to join a 'Live on Line' yoga or tai chi class, for example, to motivate you to get your body physically active. One of my friends in Scotland enjoys taking a fifteen minute yoga class on-line taught by a Brazilian lady every morning before she goes into the office. Unable to work from home this is the perfect injection of energy required to keep her mind and body balanced and focused for the day ahead. The joy of having someone halfway round the world give the instruction and enable you both to exercise 'virtually' together is half of the fun too! Everything is achievable and we can make these physical practices a part of our lives in an inexpensive way when we think more creatively about what we want to do.

Something else to be reminded of is that if you are not used to doing physical exercise and you decide to take up a class and do not like it because you take a dislike to the teacher I would encourage you to persevere with an alternative class offering a similar exercise, say yoga, and decide for yourself whether it is the type of exercise that is not a best fit for you or the fact that the style of teaching is not a best fit for you. The reason I mention this is that when I attended my first yoga class my teacher was wonderful. She never took classes over the summer, however, and as I wanted to continue taking yoga classes during this time I had to find another teacher. My friend and I attended about four different weekly classes which incorporated different styles of yoga each with different teachers until we finally found Yogi Nirmalendu whose mixed style of yoga with chanting as part of a cool down was perfect for us.

It is most important to be comfortable and able to become completely relaxed in a class with the instructor, the environment and the style of lesson delivery. This can all come together the first time you attend a class or it may take a little longer. Remember that there is a reason for everything and so even when a first class attended does not feel right for you, perhaps it will have been an opportunity for you to meet a new friend or to find out about a new café in the area that you next want to visit. Be aware and curious about what there is there for you and open up to everything that is around you wherever you go, because the universe frequently has a way of sending you information while you are focused on doing something else. For example, if you decide to attend a meditation class in a particular locale do not be surprised if you meet someone that you have not seen for a long time while you are parking your car or perhaps find a shop to purchase that unusual item that you have been seeking for ages yet previously were unable to find. The universe knows your innermost thoughts and so it can plan the potentials to ensure you have what you need and more when you go with the flow of life. One of our major tasks is to remain aware of what these opportunities may be when they are presented to us on our daily path.

Nothing beats a walk in the park or nature area. There was a Natural England survey undertaken in September 2019 that reported a disappointing 9% of children having access to nature. We as human beings are allied to nature which means that we need to participate in all things natural as part of reclaiming our balance and wholeness. Hands on experiences in a natural setting stimulate our sensate realm, especially for children. Remember that friendly bacterium

exists in soil too! Mud is ok in which to play! Simple sensory experiences from listening to the rain fall on leaves, plants and the ground to sitting on the ground and feeling the dirt beneath your bare feet enhance your sensory experience for free!

Other activities that are excellent to calm one's mind and bring focus into the physical grounding of one's energy are guided meditations, acupuncture, reiki, Indian champissage (head massage), emotional freedom tapping (EFT), a foot massage, an Ayurvedic massage, a face massage and a general massage. These can each bring restorative energy renewal and rejuvenation to your whole body that aid you in being able to open up more to your wholeness where you have been shut down. Such healing practices are for you to listen to yourself and to reconnect with your physical body. They also show you the power of your mind. When your mindset changes your physical health can come back into equilibrium. As you give intention and clear motivation for believing enough in yourself then you can achieve anything. You are worthy of being here and enjoying a great life unique to you just by being here and breathing each breath of love in the air. You exist and therefore it is your birthright to claim everything that is true about you and for you. You are dearly loved by the universe no matter what because the universe does not judge you. Love is void of judgement. When you can first learn to honour yourself and shift your thought patterns away from a blame culture, a sense of self-pity and being a victim, your energy will positively shift to a higher frequency than before. As we mature and change the way we think about life, this shows up first in our energetic vibration because everything is built on energy first before it then transmutes into our emotional and physical bodies. You are able to tap

into your own ability to heal yourself. As you start to grow in your own confidence that you are safe and secure and divinely loved simply for being here on planet earth, this assurance will start to influence the rest of your life.

Suggested Affirmations to support balance in the first chakra are:

I always feel supported, safe and nurtured by Mother Earth in my daily life.

I honour and give thanks for the anchor of the universe within my body that supports me and meets all of my needs.

I have a right to be here and feel comfortable in the physical world.

I treat my physical body as my 'sacred temple'. It is an expression of me and I love me.

I am in my life NOW and my true nature is joy.

I am ready to be led out of my old energy patterns, dear Spirit show me the way!

I am a magnificent human being worthy of enjoying a long life of joy, love and abundance.

I am love.

Once you have a balanced first chakra supplying your survival energy from Mother Earth in so many different ways from the beautiful air that you breathe to the sourcing of the food that you eat, you will be ready for this grounding energy to flow upwards to the remaining six chakras, of which the next channel of energy to be impacted is the impassioned second chakra called the Swadhistana.

CHAPTER 4

Chakra 2
Sexuality and Pleasure

Let us honour the second chakra of emotionality
As we learn to balance our feelings of sensuality
Enabling the flow and movement of our passion
To maturely sync with our ideal love vision!
~ Lady Wise

Now that you have owned your right to be here, you are entitled to relaxation and pleasure which includes sensual and sexual pleasure. The 'sweetness' of this second channel of energy which is governed by the element of water signifies to us that movement and change are fundamental expressions of how we feel, communicate our emotions and find our needs and desires satisfied within the boundaries of honouring ourselves and those with whom we share pleasure both sexual and non-sexual.

Feel the Spirit of Fun

What is true for you now that you are stepping into?
Start to feel what you need and what feels correct
for you!
It is time to reconnect with your sensate realm of pleasure
Opening up to your wholeness in peace and
graceful leisure
As you go about your daily life ask yourself what needs
forgiveness
So you can reassess and reclaim your aliveness
This second chakra is the energy path to self-gratification
With the focus on movement, sexuality and
emotional sensation
It governs the body's sacral plexus and lower abdomen
As we sense and tune into our feelings with acumen
Embrace the portal of sight, smell, sound, touch and taste
Connecting your inner world to universal space
From a healthy first chakra of grounded root energy
You are able to grow and tune into your body's
natural synergy
It is your birth right to indulge in your chosen pleasures
Set your intention to be in the spirit of fun
without measure
When you are curious and have a sense of exploration
You can move forward without hesitation
Nurtured by gravity feel the love in your play
And be guided by the desire in your heart each day!
~ Lady Wise

As we come into our choices and freewill it is important to understand where an imbalance may occur in this Sanscrit named second chakra called Swadhistana meaning 'sweetness'.

106

So often when a person reaches adolescence and indeed, long into their adult life they may encounter difficulties and/or obstacles with this chakra, specific to their sexual happiness which requires healing in order to balance this channel of energy and reignite the passion and joy of healthy sexual relationships.

Can you remember how it feels to be excited and full of exuberance? When you are able to relax you can let things develop and enjoy the experience. The ability to honour all your feelings is to accept your wholeness of being. This includes your sexual feelings and the freedom to be able to express these within a respected environment that is void of manipulation, trauma, abuse and any feelings of guilt. An harmonious, healthy second chakra will spin with liberated enthusiasm for the joy of living each new day with a freedom of spirit that is graceful, loving and capable of 'going with the flow', especially when the world around seems locked into chaos and disorder while new ways and better ways of working things out are fathomed out. I would suggest staying away from whatever makes you feel uncomfortable.

As I have already mentioned we are living throughout the Changeover Years which involves much 'shift' as we each make choices for ourselves as to what is now true for us. The developmental stage of this chakra is approximately six months to two years old. How well our second chakra has developed will depend on how our parents and close family and friends treated us during this time. If we felt loved and could sense that loving, nurturing environment then we are likely to have a strongly developed chakra. Disappointingly, many individuals as babies and young toddlers experienced traumatic family life when one or more parents suffered from an addiction, such as alcohol. All pleasure addictions

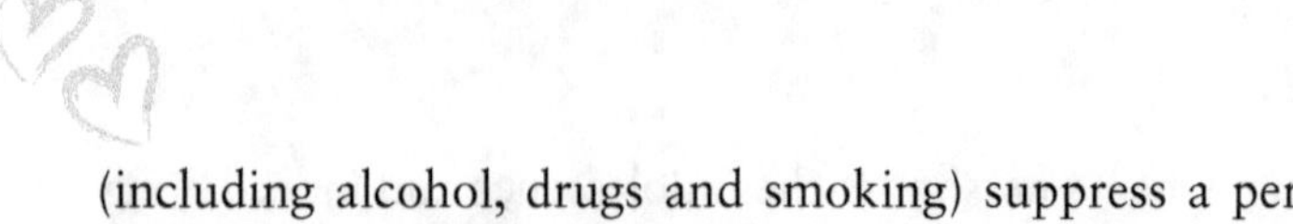

(including alcohol, drugs and smoking) suppress a person's consciousness and ability to move forward in their life.

Furthermore, the emotional dependency on which individuals come to rely, disempowers them from being capable of making sound decisions for their highest good. Any feelings from such substances are short term and artificial to that person's body and mind collectively. The disconnect from mind and body, sense and sensuality, only distances that human's connection with the divine spark that gives them their power when this evolves within a loving, caring, nourishing environment of emotional, physical and mental stability. The same holds true for any fears, abuse and feelings of separation that one has.

All addictions emanate from a buy-in to the idea that you are separate from everything. This is the 'illusion' of living in a linear world of duality. This separation causes a weakness in your energy field and has you feeling that you are powerless and a victim. It is a program deep in your physiological, cellular structure and will play games with you often with a repeat pattern that is connected to unhealed trauma, often an emotional wound. Our 'emotional body' can hold this at a cellular level but the good news is that all of our cells regenerate over a period of time and so when you can finally recognise the pattern that has been playing out in your life and come to be an observer of this, then you can start the healing journey of learning to love yourself unconditionally.

In this process of self-love, you feel a rejuvenation of your own power (which never left you but the old program that was running at an unconscious level had you believing the illusion that it had) and you regain your self-esteem and sense of self-worth. Your true power can never be separate from you! When you begin a path of unconditionally loving yourself this commences a shift in your core sense of power and who you are. You may start to feel the new energies throughout your body as the reprogramming starts across all levels of your being – energetic, mental, emotional, spiritual and physical. Healing has begun! When you shift your perception of the illusion with your intention you create a gentle rewiring in your brain. It may feel like a whole new awakening for you as you become aware and can accept the beautiful unconditional love and benevolent energies that invisibly surround you to nurture and welcome you back to your true self. Spirit knows who you are! When you can relax and respect yourself enough to honour all of your experiences across not just this lifetime but across multiple lifetimes without judgement, this helps you to balance the addiction within your chakra system. You realise that your own power is always within you. Moreover, on a daily basis you can accept 'what is' for you and develop a belief system that supports and loves you as you are – perfect in your own uniqueness.

Perhaps this may become a key area of shift for you especially in the period from May 2020 to January 2022, when the planetary alignment is supporting us to question what are our own belief systems and how do we want to show up in the world going forward into this new decade? We have a special opportunity to step into our maturity and confidence to become more child-like instead of childish in our approach to the game of life. Allow me to explain the difference using an example.

It may be that you were brought up within a very religious family to the extent that you were encouraged by your parents to ignore or to dismiss any neighbours or people with whom

you came into contact who held a different belief system of religion to yours. You may not have been encouraged to learn about other religions outside of your family's choice of religious practice. What we know and what we believe deeply shape our view of the world. Not every family brings up their children to understand both their own religious doctrine, if they have one, and that of other religions, so that they can decide when they are older what truth is right for them. There is more than one truth remember. We each have our own truth which is built up from accumulated life times and experiences. The key is to be so comfortable with your own belief systems whatever these may be (bearing in mind that these will most probably be constantly changing and evolving with the continuum of new information received by you) that you can accept other people will have different belief systems and further have a gracious understanding that they can co-exist alongside your own, by virtue of the fact that we are each so uniquely different.

Chakras one, two and three all focus on the development of self and the ego as a singular being before we learn the awareness and knowledge that we are all part of something so much bigger and that we are all connected. Childish qualities that are negatively played out through manipulation of a person, abuse of that person or any traumatisation to a person that causes them pain, anguish, grief or other adverse reactions are lower expressions of energy that have been misdirected to keep a person feeling small, insecure, emotionally immature and unable to form healthy relationships of all kinds including sexual relationships.

It may be that at a certain age an individual feels that they want to explore and widen their belief systems. They may feel that while they can respect what they have learned to

date, they want to seek out new information and understandings that help them come to terms with what holds true for them now and going forward in their life. This growth will not only give the soul an expanded perspective on which to build exciting new ways of being in the world but enable it to fulfil its potential by freeing itself of old beliefs, survival fears and values that are no longer relevant and meaningful to the person who now has many life experiences behind them not only in this lifetime but across other time lines. Deep in one's soul there is a yearning to rise up in maturity and to reclaim one's excitement and passion for living at this higher level which also attracts a child-like quality of adventure. This change is good for you and you will feel lighter of heart when you can let go such limiting beliefs and make space for new energy, new information, new people, new potentials and new ways of living life that are less of a struggle and borne out of grace and love for oneself and for others irrespective of their race, creed, colour and opinions. With a free mind from stuff and judgements, you have room for faith, hope and trust in all you do and want to do. This is very healing and healthy for you. Like a fearless warrior of light, you feel an inner confidence that anything is possible and you are no longer afraid of stepping into the unknown to live a fulfilled life of your choosing. You can proudly feel a strength of independence to do things your own way and can feel unburdened by the judgements of others who may not always appreciate how you do things. There is almost a regained, rejuvenated, refreshed child-like quality about the enthusiasm and excitement that you have about what to do next.

The prospect of new beginnings resonates within you as you clear out thoughts that are no longer relevant to you. This

removal of old ways that are no longer needed frees up space in your heart and mind for wonderful new understandings to come in. This energy of higher thinking raises your consciousness to a higher level than it has ever been before and this supports you in your own growth and soul journey. It is as if you are being lifted out of your singular ego, selfish mind state into an openness of collective understanding that believes in who you are as an individual, that supports who you are as an individual, yet always recognises that you are an integrated and valued part of humanity. Always remember that what other people think of you is none of your business. Ha!

Remember that these are exceptionally auspicious times in which we are presently living. The end of the second 26,000 year cycle called the Precession of the Equinoxes happened in 2012. This means that we have commenced another new 26,000 year cycle. In addition, we are ending the age of Pisces and entering the age of Aquarius which is all about creating a new world that recognises we are all connected, we are all equal and we are all one BIG family.

We are headed for peace on earth and for feeling more love, compassion and kindness for each other. In this way, we come together to find new creative solutions to the issues of the day and of those issues of the future. Already we have witnessed a fast-track approach to digital technology to help solve some of the initial problems identified from the first coronavirus pandemic that perhaps would otherwise have been slower to be developed and introduced. Certainly the ethos of working from home has been fast-tracked by companies who may not have considered that such a method was either necessary, possible or indeed more productive than working in an office environment. Isn't it interesting how a forced scenario can encourage individuals to step up and simply get on with learning something new in a very short space of time and even feel swayed to preferring the new opportunity once the learning of this new approach has settled down and that new practice becomes an extended 'comfort zone' for that person?

As human beings we have so much untapped potential that may seldom shine through until we find ourselves pushed into a situation in which we have to grow and learn new things, processes, systems and practices. Any fears that people had of learning how to use technology working from home have soon been quashed as a lockdown across the globe demanded new ways of working to be introduced and adopted quickly.

The second chakra of fluidity and movement relies on us being able to relax in whatever we are doing whether at work or outside of work. I frequently comment to shop tellers to enjoy their day and they reply that they are working. Who made up the rule that one cannot enjoy work? Surely with so many hours spent working it is important to be passionate about what you do? If your job is no longer fun perhaps it may be time to consider an alternative career?

When you enjoy what you do, you tend to excel at it which means that in turn this work may be very profitable and lucrative for you. If you are unhappy at work then this sadness and disillusionment will be held in your cellular structure wherever you go. This means that you are less likely to enjoy your leisure time because your Merkaba and DNA field are holding on to the negative expressions of your dissatisfaction with your job. This scenario applies to any aspect of your life whether it is relationships, home, family, career, finances or another matter.

Any mental matter that is not appropriately dealt with and acknowledged by the individual concerned will manifest into a physical ailment. This is the only way remaining that your body can express to you its dissatisfaction that you are not dealing with the issue at hand. All physical health challenges are linked to one of the seven chakras which, in turn, reveal the underlying story to any imbalance in your energetic body, your emotional body, your mental body, your spiritual body and your physical body.

The first chakra was relevant to recognising that our body is our beautiful vehicle of structure, stability and safety in which the essence of our spirit, our soul lives. It was concerned with us grounding our energy into Mother Earth and feeling strong yet relaxed.

In order for us to really feel alive the energy requires to flow freely through the body. The second chakra governs movement of energy. If we have a blocked second chakra then we will be unable to receive the necessary flowing energy through our physical body. The extent to which a person has a healthy second chakra which includes the attributes of empathy, emotional literacy, sexual health and a passion for life itself, will be impacted by the circumstances in which that person experienced childhood between the age of six months and two years old. The basic location of the second chakra is the sacral plexus, hips, lower abdomen and the sexual organs.

During this important part of our formative years, it is imperative that we were allowed to be independent in our crawling and walking in order to realise that as that young child, we were separate from our mother and not part of our mother's physical existence. Yet, for such a little person to feel secure in their exploration of this amazing new world of aliveness, their parents would have had to be very supportive, loving, nurturing, patient and gentle with them. There is an amplification of emotional energies and feelings which need to be allowed to be expressed in a healthy way. Touch is vital to develop sensory receptors. When feelings are suppressed then eventually the body becomes numb to what it truly feels from moment to moment and the element of this second chakra which is represented by water, is unable to flow with ease and grace through the body. The child would then become stuck in their decision making and their confidence would become depleted as a result of their inability to experience what gives them joy and is pleasurable.

If a young child was rejected or neglected by their family then this lack of supportive love and nurturing may adversely affect the child's emotional intelligence. Furthermore, it may lead to an inability to express their true feelings and successfully have loving relationships and healthy sexual relationships when they are older.

All child-hood experiences tend to remain with that person when they grow up unless they become sufficiently aware to understand what events took place in their child-hood and can work through the necessary release of any trauma experiences and heal from them. It is only with the much needed healing and understanding of their young lives' experiences that they will be able to make progress in going forward in their life with a balanced Swadhisthana.

We are here to get to know ourselves better at an energetic and experiencial level so that we can fulfil our dreams and passions. When a person has experienced a traumatic childhood in these early years and/or has been repressed and/ or discouraged from walking for example, then this leaves

very deep programming within that person's energy field which needs to be positively transformed to reverse the imbalance.

Similarly if a person was subjected to emotional, mental or physical abuse perhaps as a young child due to an alcoholic parent then that person as an adult may carry much guilt that has been projected on to them inappropriately. The programs and energy effectively require to be reworked so that the individual does not repeat the old programming of believing in and only doing things a certain way.

A belief that you hold, may not be the truth. The extent to which you have been indoctrinated with this belief from your parents, for example, makes you think that this belief must be the truth but it may not be once you take the time to research that belief further and start to question and challenge it.

When a child has been exposed to domestic violence or experienced another type of 'troubled childhood' of which sadly there are many stories, this second chakra may not develop in a balanced way.

Specific to this channel of energy there may be physical issues that manifest with that child in later life especially those of a sexual nature which occur because of a fear based childhood. Feelings of helplessness perhaps about a situation and/or because the child was forced to repress their emotions at such an early age may mean that they do not have the program to express themselves in adulthood either. These individuals have been unable to develop this part of their chakra system in a normal way and so health challenges that may exist include the following in no particular order:-

- A person's lack of desire for food and/or sexual pleasure and in extreme cases a complete disinterest in their personal well-being and in wanting to be alive because of dulled senses and finding one's life dull;

- Sexual frustrations and sexual disorders/dissatisfaction affecting the reproductive organs including premature ejaculation; frigidity; impotence; inability to have an orgasm, menstrual issues;

- Knee ailments and

- An overall lack of flexibility in one's body movements.

We need to be honest with ourselves about what our true values are from the perspective of our heart rather than our logical mind. You are never given an experience that is too much for you, but similarly there is no more need to feel like a victim and to accept any form of suffering in your life anymore.

It is time for any bubble of victimhood or guilt that you feel from your life experiences to date to be burst wide open for you to realise that you have the power within you to take back full control over your reality and the creativity of what you want to do and how you want to live your life from a greater, more expanded joy-filled state of being. Allow the beauty and strength of your intuition, your inner guidance system to steer you to action everything that is good for you and to reignite your passion for life and aliveness.

Remember that you are a spiritual being experiencing physical life on this planet for a short time in the vessel or

vehicle of your physical body. Why would you not want to lighten up and live your best life? You decide! You can choose to live an harmonious and balanced life. It only takes three seconds to change one's mind. When you start to take charge of your feelings, you are able to stand up for your feelings and know that you do not need to seek another person's approval to express the essence and energy of who you are. Be gentle with yourself and be kind to yourself as you work out new ideas, new solutions and new programming to expand your beautiful inner light. The divine spark of creativity that is within you simply wants to shine and show the world your uniqueness, beauty and have you feel the inner peace inside your whole being that comes from being in balance and confident in allowing the flow of life to pass through you energetically and fill you up with passion and a desire that is full-hearted, true for you and empowering. Only you can discover all the strength that is inside of you to propel you forward to accomplish great things and thrive!

When the second chakra is out of balance, once again the reason may be due to:-

- a deficiency;

- an excess in that chakra or

- a combination of both a deficiency reason and an excess reason.

Some of the deficiencies that may arise have just been identified as health challenges. It is time to reconnect with your passion and pleasure in living life and so if you have been in denial about the pleasure of which you are deserving, then this may indicate that your second chakra is slightly

deficient. Joy is sacred and there is no reason why we should not be enjoying our life every single day.

Recently when I was shopping in a supermarket, the store manager acknowledged me on the way into the store and commented on my apparent happiness. He asked if I was always so joyful and I laughingly replied,'Yes.' Before he had a chance to say another word I picked up his body language and further explained that I realised that my own joy could sometimes be most annoying to those individuals who preferred to be miserable especially first thing in the morning. Ha! He then laughed and I walked on down the aisle.

Know that at any time you can choose your spiritual will over your ego will. Rather than being fearful of change why not consider a little shift in your thinking that perhaps there may be something better for you than your present situation?

A deficient second chakra always wants to hide behind fear and this fear can make an individual feel very fixed about what they do without being adaptable and flexible to new choices and new ways of doing things.

We need Gaia to survive and yet sadly we seldom acknowledge her very presence because we have been living in ignorance of all the wonder that is free around us! The presence of Gaia is absolutely necessary for our very existence but because both love and air are invisible we tend to forget their power.

How can we harness this power to make it work for us? It starts with the art of choice and what you choose to create, think, say and do.

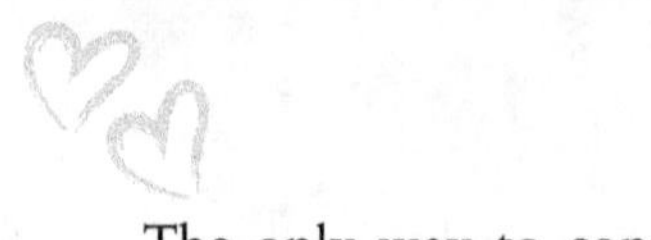

The only way to connect with your own 'love power' and divine essence that is inside of you is through the power of love.

Whenever you wake up and feel troubled about anything or feel low because someone has belittled you in front of others, ridiculed you or even ignored you, take a deep breath and remember from the core of your heart that spirit sees you as perfect...in every way!

You are a magnificent human being whose life is so precious. Each of us is on a spiritual quest, whether we realise it or not, and this life quest takes us along many paths of our own choosing with the opportunity to meet friends and acquaintances, old and new, and to learn, love and laugh along the way. When you encounter anyone or anything along your path that makes you feel uncomfortable, then sharpen up in your awareness and think for yourself why you are feeling uncomfortable. Is it perhaps because you are unhappy about being in a particular person's company who is unappreciative or disrespectful of you? Is it because you feel you are being put in a position that does not feel true to your beliefs and choices that you want to make or is it for another reason?

Remember, that where each of us stands today is as a result of all of the choices we have made in our life to date. Sometimes when we look closely at where we are and what we are doing now, we receive a reality check that makes us feel that there is more to our precious life than we ever thought about before. Some individuals have an epiphany and realise that perhaps a career shift is required, or a change in personal relationships is necessary, or that a long forgotten childhood dream that was never fulfilled, resurfaces in one's

mind and the inner drive to achieve this demands a change in future choices made.

Often, thoughts occur to us that small changes could be made to make us feel happier. Perhaps a change in the type of food that you feel you want to eat occurs to you or an idea pops into your mind to go for a walk in nature or along the nearest beach instead of sitting in front of the television. Do not ignore your first intuitive thought! It may be a fleeting glimpse but it may be an important choice which leads you to inner peace, calm and happiness amidst these chaotic and challenging times! You cannot make a mistake when you make a choice about anything, because spirit sees you as perfect and so, take a good look in the mirror and learn to love yourself for who you are today. Trust and believe that you can make great choices for yourself and that you are the best person to make choices for yourself because you are one of a kind and know yourself better than any other person!

Affirmations are a wonderful way to help you on your way. May I suggest the following affirmation for you today:

"

Everything works out better than I imagined!

As you become more aware of your feelings, you will slowly improve on the choices that you make for yourself. When you choose to live a life filled with joy, love and laughter and focus on making choices that give you this outcome, watch for subtle changes that may occur for the better. You may find, for example, that you are laughing more each day, you feel happier in yourself, you feel less anxious about issues, you make more time for spending with other friends

and family members whose company you enjoy and who make you feel loved and respected too!

It all starts with that look in the mirror and the acceptance of who you are today. From this you can go at your own pace to improve the art of choosing what makes you happy! In as little as three seconds you can choose to change a situation/scenario that is not working for you and take a different life path! Only you can do this for yourself. When you can first love yourself with all your heart then the love that you can give to others is pure love. When you still carry negative energies and old energy patterning such as anger, jealousy and greed, then you are limiting yourself in your ability to simply be a wholly loving human being. You are also restricting the divine essence of love that is within you, that waits for you to awaken to the marvel of who you are in all your uniqueness and magnificence.

Learn to relax and reassure yourself that only good things are coming your way! Live in honesty and truth from your heart. Believe that you have the necessary wisdom, help and support for facing a difficult situation.

You deserve to be joyful! Love yourself enough to find balance within a peaceful mind and you can achieve all that you want in life.

All we need to do is relax and allow the synchronicity of potentials to play out with everyone concerned. Remember, there are more than seven billion human beings on the planet and so this is a lot of 'potentials' for spirit to organise for each of us at exactly the right time in the right place.

Your very existence is light for the planet. Open your heart to good vibrations and trust in good intentions! Reconnect with the joy of experiencing your feelings and share this joy with your family, friends and your extended family and work colleagues. Be yourself because you are different!

Feel the essence of love deep within your heart. You are never alone! The universe has your back. It is no coincidence that more than 80% of the planet believes that there is something more to us than our physical body.

Let your joy, curiosity and expectation, open you up to revelation! Expect the unexpected! The more you can allow yourself permission to be who you truly are, the more you give others permission to be themselves too! Listen to your intuition for what is best for you and FEEL the right answer! Respect the past and create the new! All life thrives with LOVE!

So what can be done to heal and restore balance to this second chakra? Movement and emotion are essential to restoring the flow of energy throughout one's body for balance and healing. When energy is trapped in a chakra or multiple chakras in the body then a side effect may be pain. It is important for you to pay attention to how you are feeling.

Suggested Affirmations to support balance in the second chakra are:

I am worthy of enjoying myself and undertake pleasurable pursuits.

I am enthusiastic about life and I have a healthy sense of pleasure.

I always make time for physical pleasure and enjoy connecting with the senses and feelings in my body.

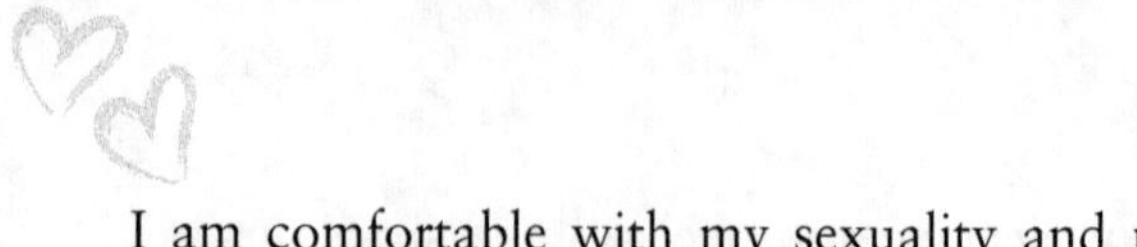

I am comfortable with my sexuality and maintain healthy emotional and sexual boundaries.

I am emotionally secure and my happiness, intimacy and joy come from nurturing myself and others.

I am protected from danger and trust my own senses to guide me with ease and grace in my passion for life.

I am living my life guilt free and honour my sacred body.

When you improve the understanding and flow of your own inner matrix of energy you will be amazed at how your own well-being improves and how much better you are able to get along with others. The second chakra is focused on feeling the energy that pulsates around your body and instinctively trusting your senses to avoid any shutdown of the sensate realm that is likely to then restrict you in your choices going forward.

While the first chakra's attribute was that of matter centred on feeling safe and secure, the second chakra's attribute of movement has concentrated on becoming centred in our pleasure. Let us now take these two chakras serving the basic instinctual needs of a human being and add to the earth and water of chakras one and two respectively, the fire element to invite some propelled action and power in our being.

CHAPTER 5

Chakra 3
Feeling Confident

"

Challenges greet us as we move forward into the unknown
We move into our multiplicity and rise up from our
safe home
Our understanding suitably tempers the sparks of
consciousness fire
Transforming our energy to will and achieve our desire!
~ Lady Wise

Often there is no reason to change unless something happens. Generally, humans do not like change. We are reluctant to embrace change and enjoy the sameness of life each day. With the current health challenges across the globe there is a health crisis, economic crisis and financial crisis. The light that will come from this will be that of hope. We are being forced into scenarios to innovate and create new ways of doing things. We always have the choice to replace what we no longer want with higher vibrational choices of what we do want.

Within approximately eight weeks of the global pandemic announcement it is believed that many organisations and individuals managed to leap the equivalent of about five years in technological advancement in order to meet the safeguard demands of working from home, while still continuing to do effective business.

Furthermore, for example, we observed the Mercedes Formula 1 team rise to the need for ventilators and use a team to design what was necessary as their contribution to saving lives. One personal trainer in England helped to deliver food to the elderly. A Japanese whisky company used their American subsidiaries to produce bottles of sanitiser for those people working in the health services and the police. This is a paradigm shift. New awareness among human beings is creating new ways of thinking and feeling. Profound connections all across the globe are being made as hearts join together across oceans and we are making each day anew for ourselves, filled with love.

"

When you have the maturity to hold spring time in
your heart
You never feel alone from the creative source and your
own divine spark
There will always be disagreements but human nature
is changing
Every lifetime's layer of experience gifts us the opportunity
to change our reality and create healing!
~ Lady Wise

Illness is connected to an emotional body. Love is in every cell of your body. When you have a diagnosis of an ailment or suffer from a mild health challenge, this physical manifestation has transpired because you have overlooked an issue internally.

ANY PHYSICAL MANIFESTATION OF AN AILMENT IS AN EXPRESSION OF WHAT YOU NEED TO ADDRESS. Your innate knows exactly what your body needs. Your innate is one part of your non-visible, higher dimensional DNA that is packed into your Merkaba.

There is no need to complain about anything because you have the power within to be perfectly healthy. Trust that your heart knows the truth. Believe in yourself! It is your ego that will tell you otherwise.

"

You can change your biology. Consciousness being energy can actually imbue itself into the cells of your body and speak to the disease and say, 'You are inappropriate here' and they'll soon get the message.
~ Kryon

Learn to love yourself as you are. A positive attitude will help you reach your goals. Start writing your future and become a no-limit person. Follow and listen to your inner intuitive guidance. Watch what you say about others and shape your words for a great future. You are defined by your every word. Every word that you think and say is a reflection of you. I often remind myself with the words:-

"

Be unique
Be authentic
Be YOURSELF!

In this way you will have a stronger connection to your family and friends and those with whom you work. They will observe and feel the authenticity with which you speak. This in turn will bring you greater joy as your own dreams manifest. When you can learn to love and respect yourself, others will learn to love and respect you in return.

This information is for you to discern and work with yourself. Only you can discover the inner power of who you truly are.

Play is essential! It is rejuvenating and enhancing to play and to feel joyous in whatever you are doing. All illness stems from emotionally blocked energy. When you play you are enhancing your body's immune system and from this you will gain good health and freedom. Your energy levels will be naturally restored.

Some of the physical ailments that can arise when this chakra is imbalanced may be as follows:-

Fatigue in general may be symptomatic of a variety of issues that have accumulated over many years and so there is an inherent despair that no solutions have yet been found; an overall disheartening of the soul would give rise to low energy levels and a distinct lack of one's mojo or motivation; there may also be a feeling of extreme emptiness in one's life and within oneself even when that individual is fortunate to seemingly have every outward desire fulfilled and be leading an affluent lifestyle;

Hypertension may occur when a person puts themselves under undue pressure. This may be to do with work, pleasure, the extent to which they can receive and give love authentically without 'faking' their relationships. Alternatively it may concern the extent to which a person can control their anger and avoid 'letting off steam'! This holding back of one's inner tortuous feelings can lead to the physical manifestation of health challenges. At a deep level that person then feels suppressed from holding back their emotions yet at the same time is confused and unsure how to control any potential outbursts of temper. Sometimes the bottling up of these unexpressed thoughts and feelings adds to the nervous tension that is building up in that person's mind. An individual may also be prone to hyperactivity to take their mind off the stress and tension that has built up;

Diabetes involves levels of sugar in the body and this translates into the sweetness with which we embrace our life. There are so many different scenarios that may play out specific to this ailment, but they usually centre on the inability to feel joy, affection and love because of extreme sadness from say, a childhood event, a bereavement, a family disagreement that has turned sour where there is inner turmoil and resistance to resolving it or a situation in which a person feels complete despair and yet their ego drive will not allow them to detach from the past and enable them to open their heart to the love that is around them and for them to be able to receive as a sacred human being;

Eating disorders such as bulimia, anorexia or obesity stem from an unwillingness to love oneself as is, and of a reluctance to be accepting of the gift and adventure of life. These health challenges are often accompanied by great feelings of loss, stress, depression and insecurity as a result of an imbalance in the ability to understand that the universe is beautiful, loving and supportive of every human being. We simply have to understand this to restore the imbalance, but that may not be as straight forward as it seems.

Problems with one's digestion represent an uneasiness with one's life in some way. An ingredient of love will spark wonders in one's life to restore balance and harmony. It will encourage you to reconnect with your mojo and innermost dreams. I am, however, referring to your inner 'love power' and not the love that you seek from someone else. This soul journey of transformation is about you remembering the power and beauty of who you are as an individual and unique soul on this planet. When you turn inwards and listen to the whispers of your inner voice you are reminded of the magnificent being that you are. An understanding develops which opens you up to the awareness that your life existence is so much more than the external world of delusion in which you have been living.

The possible reasons for a chakra being out of balance may be due to:-

- A deficiency;

- An excess in that chakra or

- A combination of both a deficiency reason and an excess reason.

What is particularly beautiful about the element of this lustrous gem or 'Manipura' chakra specifically at this time, is that in order to attain our full power we must be willing to step out into the unknown with an adventurous spirit and have confidence in ourselves to be the change that we want to be. In recent years, I decided to write books and to write songs too, regardless of how many people would ultimately read and hear them respectively. These hobbies bring me tremendous joy and a great hope that perhaps even one person might resonate with these and feel inspired to take their own leap of faith!

So how may you be feeling if you have a deficient third chakra? You may not be feeling particularly enthusiastic about life and want to shut yourself away from social contact. The excitement of spontaneity may be absent from your daily life and you may be stuck in a 'victim' mentality wondering why the world is happening to you and blaming everyone else rather than yourself when things do not go to your plan (which of course is an 'illusion', yet a very real one to you when you are in this mindset). At the extreme, you may feel severely lethargic and unresponsive to anyone helping you out of your lassitude. You may feel hopeless and powerless instead of feeling alive and hopeful about what each new day can bring you.

In addition, you may be very poor at making any kind of decision because you even mistrust your own decision-making and feel totally confused and isolated about what to do next. This mistrust may extend to you becoming an unreliable person with your family, friends and/or work colleagues who have no idea about the sadness and melancholy that lies within you about what to do with your life and your inability of being able to understand why you are in this situation at this time. Perhaps you feel that life is very unfair and you feel 'blocked'. Sometimes these thoughts of low self-esteem are rooted in shame issues and/or excessive anger that have built up which have been unable to be released in a healthy way to allow you to move forward with your life. Remember that all of these feelings may have built up not just from this lifetime but across many lifetimes and time lines. When this happens it can easily add confusion to you because you struggle to find the reason for where you are now in this lifetime and often discount other lifetimes and time cycles as major contributors to how you feel and the unhealed

trauma which has manifested in a variety of physical health challenges for you.

When an individual experiences an excessive third chakra, possible symptoms of this may show up as follows:-

- Arrogance;

- Antagonistic;

- Strong competitiveness and a desire to win at all costs even through deceitful and manipulative means;

- A strong need to be right and to always have the last word in a discussion or conversation;

- Someone who is prone to aggressive outbursts and temper tantrums;

- Hyperactivity;

- Extreme selfishness;

- Extreme stubbornness.

In a severe case, an excessive third chakra may also explain why a person has an attraction to sedatives.

So what can be done to heal and restore balance to this third chakra?

The power of our will is what drives us forward to attain whatever it is that we wish. When we remain in an unhealthy ego state, however, we can become so selfishly obsessed with our own goals and ambition that we become disconnected from the wider social community. Moreover, we may forget our responsibility to question whether this is for our highest good and the highest good of those involved in achieving our success.

We have been taught to judge others in an environment of duality. This approach is unhealthy and cannot continue for each of us to become empowered and to empower one another. It is imperative for us to learn to honour ourselves first and to honour the differences of the opinions of others too. We are all equal. When we choose to a life based on true love, that love is unconditional. True love is! True love transcends duality and lives in a quantum reality. With maturity, we can learn how to transcend the reality of duality and to experience life from a higher reality lived with a loving heart that is compassionate and caring. Are you still with me? Yes there are multiple realities in which we can thrive. There is more than the one reality of duality which has its basis in a low energy of limitation, selfishness and separation. Perception is everything!

Furthermore, most of us have been brought up to obey rules and procedures often without questioning and challenging the appropriateness of these. All rules are man-made. The criteria under which certain rules were originally constructed may now have significantly changed and yet no review of these regulations has been undertaken to address a change in circumstances. Remember that you always have the right to question something that does not sit comfortably with you. You are nobody's slave. Take back your responsibility (that is, your ability to respond) and challenge accordingly.

The purpose of this chakra is to allow you to recognise your individuality and to act on your will without feeling inhibited, restricted, limited or shamed from another. It is for us all to learn to behave nobly and from a balanced perspective of integrity, love and compassion.

Whenever I mention the importance of individual empowerment and an individual connecting with their true sense of power I am referring specifically to that attribute of 'power-with'. Disappointingly, this has not always been understood by those in my company over recent years. I can recall one occasion when I was at an interview for an interesting corporate role and the two interviewers looked at one another aghast when I mentioned the word 'empowerment'. It was clear to me that they were confusing the traditional model of 'power-over' rather than the new paradigm model of 'power-with'. Consequently, I was unsurprised when I was not offered the job. Ha!

For clarity on these two power models, an out of date 'power-over' model has the attributes of control, subjugation, intimidation, superiority over another and competitive struggle and 'win-over' at the expense and detriment of others. To this end, there is the perception that the victor in the 'struggle' has become powerful while the loser has become powerless. So many of the 'isms' in our fragmented society such as sexism, racism and ageism are the output from this narrow-minded thought process. It is time for change!

In the energy of the Shift and the new paradigm of an evolving humanity with maturity and wisdom, the focus is on a 'power-with' model. This 'lustrous gem' energy of the Manipura chakra is centred on each human choosing to tap into their power within. What is power? How can we structure it for positive influence and still feel positively enlivened from its use?

Are you remembering that everything is energy? We are energy. We are such magnificent human beings and for as much as we have the power to destroy, we have the power

to create and nurture from a place of love and playfulness. The choice of how you use your power is entirely up to you. The reason the 'Old Souls' are here is to use their power in an assertive and confident way instead of in an aggressive and conflictive manner.

As with all duality and polarity there is always the option of a higher or a lower expression to the choices that we make. The lower expressions are always based on the low energy of a person while the higher expressions emanate from a person who is maturing and has a sense of the bigger life picture for themselves and others.

No-one needs to live in a state of fear. When you live from such a low energy vibration the power of your thinking brings to you what is on your mind. What is true for you? How easily can you learn how to live with other people having different opinions to you? You choose how you view life. This is all about your own internal journey to appreciate your own sacredness first. Therein, one is able to recognise the love in others regardless of their opinions, views and differences. From this perspective we empower one another.

Everyone has had wounds.

"

Turn your wounds into wisdom.
~ Oprah Winfrey

Specific to this third chakra is the ability to rise up from the lower expression of believing that you are a 'victim' of life and transforming your situation by exerting a positive mindset over matter and truly believing in yourself to

assertively claim your place on this earth as a uniquely loved human being. All hatred, frustration, anxiety and worry when outwardly talked out or written down, for example, serve as a healing.

It is so important to be able to live in the present moment and to be accepting of who you are and where you are right now in this moment. We can learn to never give up and to find a way through the 'stickiness' of our life. What has happened in the past has forever gone. Of course there are reminders that can cause an emotional response in each of us. Music is very powerful for this. When we are in full power and full control, however, we have peace in our heart and live totally in the present moment.

So many people have taken the opportunity throughout lockdown to look at their internal world. They have learned how this can be wonderful for healing old wounds and growing in spirituality and maturity. We can send prayers to help heal one another. What a unique time to explore the power of our thoughts, emotions and mental strength! The highest expression of this chakra is to transform one's energy into a daily joy of living, enthusiastic to embrace our strengths and weaknesses as these envelop our individuality propelling us forward with a dynamic inner 'love power' that inspires both us and those with whom we meet along our transformational soul journey of life.

When we learn to take more responsibility for our actions, we are able to confidently respond to scenarios rather than react weakly to them.

Suggested Affirmations to support balance in the third chakra are:

I take responsibility for myself and have a clear sense of my own power.

I am able to prioritise my desires and discipline myself to fulfil them.

I am willing to take on challenges with a sense of high self-esteem.

I feel full of energy and achieve things with ease and grace.

I believe in myself and understand that I am not what I do.

I am enthusiastic about my life and want to do things.

I am self-assured and do not give away my personal power to others.

I am spontaneous and make time for playfulness in my daily routine.

I am strong with high self-worth.

I enjoy new challenges with confidence.

Remember what brings you joy, again and again and again. Observe how differently people with whom you come into contact will react to you when you live from a place of joy and love all the time! If you are an animal lover then observe how animals respond to you whether these are domestic or wild animals. When you live in joy, your whole being resonates with a beautiful, higher vibration, which is recognised by animals and birds. They know that you have changed and will want to spend more time around you. When you are lost for inspiration may I suggest you look to nature!

"
When did you last walk in nature among creatures?
We are in an alliance with Mother Earth as our teacher
Be forever open to the pleasures of life
Set a new course of love without strife
Listen to your messages from the sensate realm
Stride confidently forward and take your place at the helm
This planet is waiting to be greeted by you
As you tune in to love and joy that is true!
~ Lady Wise

CHAPTER 6

Chakra 4
Perfect Love

"

The path of self-love is where this rich journey begins
May a sense of calm connect you to your true
power within
Unconstrained by your ability to be kind and to forgive
You will become filled with the love of all that lives!
~ Lady Wise

Hello to love and free hearts! You did not come to earth to suffer, to be sad, to be in pain or to be poor. That is not the plan. The plan for humanity is with free will to reconnect with the creator source, God, spirit, Higher Self, your soul or that which is by another name. You have been born to recognise your alliance with Mother Nature and to feel confident, comfortable and secure in who you are, able to talk about your problems when appropriate and to be enthusiastic about your well-being. Good health is your strong foundation from which you are transformed with a

renewed purpose to fulfil your desires without any need to suppress your feelings or to feel intimidated by anyone.

What matters to you in the long term? When you put in the time to take a good look at yourself there is an opportunity to make a permanent life change that helps you build new energy for personal commitments, priorities and understandings. What are you capable of doing as your possible 'best self'?

Simply by finding your balance and being slow to anger and more compassionate and at peace with yourself, will not only have resounding positive repercussions for you, but you will also be helping those with whom you come into contact around you to feel more balanced and calm too! It's a win, win for all!

Unless you can become a balanced person you will limit the extent to which you can do most things. I appreciate that on occasion it can be very challenging to be balanced when there is chaos, noise and nonsense as I call it going on around you, but this will flow when your life is based in love, you live from your heart and trust in the process of love. When you do this, you connect in a higher way that will make your life easier.

We are learning to raise our consciousness and to connect and experience a universal love for which we yearn. There is a vitality in human life which is the power of life itself. It is available to everyone to tap into and enjoy, yet it is only attainable when we can each learn first to love and respect ourselves. Is this too straight forward for you?

Now is the time for us to lighten up, share our hearty laughter, find time to relax and recognise the life energy that is present in everything. Nature is a wonderful nurturer and elevator to make us feel more true to who we are. The beauty of a natural landscape can powerfully soothe our hearts, help us to unwind and inspire us. In your emotional world your feelings are your truth. Gift yourself the time, energy and effort to take responsibility to make the necessary changes for you to feel happy and contented within your heart. Be aware of where you are putting your energy. Remember that we are effectively taking our past lives and present life to recreate our future, in a higher vibrational frequency of love.

When you are able to view everything that happens in your life from a place of love, it will positively transform your outlook and bring you solutions to all those areas of discomfort and anxiety. The love and respect that you build for yourself provides you with the protective light shield that you need. Are you remembering that happy people have a strong immune system? One of the greatest gifts you can give yourself is the patience and faith to trust that the universe always has your back and wants to work with you to give you the best life possible. All you require to do is to follow the way of your heart. Give yourself the credit you deserve. When you learn to trust yourself you naturally live your life more spontaneously. The energy flows through your body with vitality and you are able to accept change is constant. With your new found freedom of thought and actions you feel inspired to connect with others who are like-minded, playful and who laugh often! Are you willing to call in a new truth for you that lets you feel protected and safe even in the worst times of uncertainty? There is a phrase that I regularly use to help keep me centred which is,

When you continuously live from a core truth that only the best possible outcomes are waiting for you, then it gives you an incredible peace of mind.

Awareness is the key to the evolution of humanity and inner peace. When you hold the thought of peace...you are peace.

The essence of this fourth chakra whose Sanscrit name is Anahata is to feel that you are loved and to love. Your ability to learn how to accept and love yourself will permanently shift your consciousness. This, in turn, will help you to accept others as they are because everyone matters!

The location of this energy centre is the heart, chest and cardiac plexus. Is it any wonder that the tenderness of this chakra is very vulnerable to wounding in the form of grief, betrayal, conditional love and abuse? These are just a few traumas which can cause the misalignment of these pockets of nerve ganglia. Due to the sensitivity of our hearts and our need for love, when we reject our feelings and emotions of the heart and fail to unite our mind and body, the physical manifestations that often result are heart attacks, general heart disorders and cardiac problems.

In addition, asthma, circulatory issues, disorders of the breasts, lungs and arms may manifest. These disorders can occur because an individual does not feel stable in their life circumstances and in control. Sometimes a person can have suffered so many disappointments in their lifetime that they have lost faith in the power of love and struggle to receive love as well as to be able to forgive themselves and truly love themselves for the unique soul of wonder that they are.

Our hearts represent love. The position of this fourth chakra of the heart lies at the centre of the seven chakras making up this rainbow bridge journey of the soul. It is the central point where the balance of the divine feminine with the divine masculine occurs. Any distortion of this harmony, however, has an adverse impact on one's mental and emotional stability.

The lower expressions or vibrations of love may show up in different ways. Some examples are as follows:- jealousy; possessiveness due to an insecurity about one's own life; co-dependency; demanding relationships or a fragility about setting defined boundaries.

If you can relate to any of these examples given perhaps it is time to have some 'alone time' to rethink your priorities and identify what really matters to you. Be alert and aware of the importance of both the emotional side of how you are feeling and your rational, logical mind which require to come together in balance to provide you with the love, strength and protection required for happiness in your everyday life.

We seriously need to take care of our hearts. This magnificent organ is the most magnetic of all our organs and is critical to the three–way connection of the heart, mind and pineal gland to the universal mind of all that is – the creative source, God, spirit or by whatever preferred name you would like to call it.

When this chakra becomes out of balance, as with the other chakras, it may be due to:-

- A deficiency;

- An excess in that chakra or

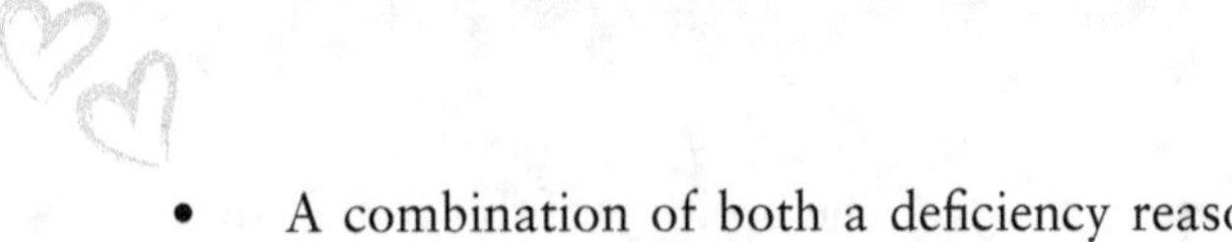

- A combination of both a deficiency reason and an excess reason.

A deficient heart energy centre may show itself in a person as someone who is in a depressive state and considers that they are a helpless victim where life is always a struggle for them. They may feel very dejected and want to isolate themselves away from everyone even although they may feel extreme loneliness in doing this. Indeed, an individual's inability to find a reason for living may arise from childhood trauma or the death of a loved one which is almost all consuming that person's mind and preventing them from seeing the good things that are happening to them. It is as if the mind is cloaking them in a dark cloud of negativity and they are no longer able to see clearly the direction of their life ahead.

There may also be such a disbelief in that person recognising their own capability that they feel rejected by life and empty inside without strength and a purpose to go on. These feelings accumulate when a person has massive unhealed trauma inside them from drama that has happened to them perhaps not just in this present lifetime, but across lifetimes. It requires a healing of their soul at a deep level. Everything is possible to heal this state. It starts with one's next breath and an inner knowingness that you have all that you need inside of you to heal. You are so beautifully unique as a soul and a human being and when you can give yourself one chance to relax and go with the flow of life, instead of feeling that you have to force certain situations, you can begin to give yourself the space you need and the trust you need, to move beyond feeling stuck. You are able to reconnect with your inner voice that will reassure you that you have a purpose on this earth and that THE UNIVERSE KNOWS WHO YOU ARE BY NAME.

Sometimes the dissatisfaction that one feels with one's life is due to a deep rooted fear. These fears can throw the heart chakra into imbalance. There are those who have a fear of relationships, a fear of loss, a fear of taking responsibility or perhaps a fear of intimacy. The truth is there are so many fears that I am unable to mention them all but hopefully if you are reading this book and you have a fear of something then this paragraph will trigger your own fear(s) and you may start to become aware of how you are not alone and can choose to start paying attention to your heart and your body and to see a solution to your situation. The universe loves YOU! There may be many unresolved situations in your life and you always have the choice to make peace with them and to forgive yourself. This is an awesome opportunity for you to simply be in the present moment and know that you have all the necessary strength within you to turn your life around for a better, happier, more abundant YOU!

Other deficiencies with this chakra may manifest themselves as an intolerance of others and someone who is very judgemental of others. In essence, this is a mode of deflection from oneself. Any aspect or attribute we perceive in another person we perceive in ourselves. If someone is described as cold-hearted then that person would be open to changing something to correct the imbalance that exists. Often, however, we all have to work harder at listening. Every person with whom we come into contact is like a mirror reflection of our own personality at any level. There is kindness, joy and love in all of us. When you see a happy person and criticise them for always being so joyful, this is you choosing to reject the part of yourself that could be happy too. When you can step back from this judgement (which keeps you in duality like a restrained wild bird that is caged) and instead of passing comment simply 'be' with what you are seeing, you will come to realise that a subtle shift in how you think may transform your own dissatisfied life...in an instant, if you want it to. This is the incredulous and transformative power of the universe in which we are presently living, as Mother Earth continues her travels through the Precession of the Equinoxes. THIS IS THE TIME TO BE ALIVE! This is the time to fast-track your own journey to good health, abundance and love because of all the unique and abundant invisible loving energies that are continually pouring into this planet waking humanity up to its evolution and maturity for a new world of living in freedom, peace and love. Just sit with this thought and FEEL IT FOR YOURSELF!

"

Allow the joy of new life to enter your heart
Feel the sweet bliss of nature that will nourish
a new start
You have the fibre of a hero within
Feel guided to banish fear and never give in!
~ Lady Wise

Astrologically, the alignment of the planets is such that we are going to start to SEE what has been hidden from humanity and 'in the dark'. We are headed for peace, balance and a life of trust. Always remember your inner voice is the best voice to listen to. Your intuition and your gut feeling never let you down. First, the lesson is to love yourself and trust yourself. This will bring you great inner strength and start to positively change your whole energetic and DNA cellular structure. A happy heart is a healthy heart!

Our heartbeat is part of the universal heartbeat...
but you have to learn to participate in the dance.
~ Osho

The Big ASK! You deserve to be loved and to be helped. The golden universal rule is that every human has free choice. This means that you have to ask for the loving guidance that you need, otherwise all the angels and your entourage team who are always around you are not allowed to help you. There is no right way to ask. In whatever way you decide to ask, this will be perfect – no judgement! Some suggestions may be to do this in your mind, by asking aloud, or by writing the request on a piece of paper.

Hey, creative source, sorry I took so long.
I am asking for help.

You will do it your way and that will be best for you. It's easy! You always have your freedom of choice!

A person who is lacking in empathy and who comes across as withdrawn and quite antisocial may have imbalances with their heart chakra. An individual can cut themselves off from receiving and giving affection because of the pressure that they put themselves under and the daily stress of life about facing up to what may come their way. One of the biggest lessons many of us learn is that your life does not lose meaning when you fail at something. In fact, this can often be the biggest catalyst and opportunity for you to explore hidden gifts that you didn't know you had. The universe gifts you the time to be able to tap into more of who you

are without feeling your life is being run by what other people say to you.

One gentleman who found himself redundant after many years working at a global company now has a fulfilled life producing remarkable still life oil paintings. His passionate work has been heralded as comparable to paintings by the great Dutch masters! Every one of us is being challenged in this decade to discover what our passion is and to use this as a key driver in our happiness at work and at home with family and friends.

Attributes of an excessive heart chakra show up as children and adults who are very clingy and needy in a relationship. They may even fantasise about the extent of true love in a relationship. The developmental stage of the heart chakra is between four and seven years old. Issues of imbalance that occur in a child may be carried into adulthood, before an adult can understand what life experiences have contributed to this imbalance and the trauma and/or abuse can be healed.

So many children are exposed to manipulated messages of love as children which require to become untangled in adulthood for that person to surrender to their own true feelings, reconnect with the core truth of love and of who they are as a beautiful, sacred human being. Each of us needs to learn to get to know the mystery that is our own vulnerable, authentic self! Know that you are always enough just as you are!

The previously mentioned low vibrational attributes of jealousy and co-dependency exemplify an excessive fourth chakra imbalance. These lower expressions of how we use our energy are also referred to as the shadow side to a person. In coming to better understand ourselves at a deeper level, we are able to identify with these lower expressions of how we react to situations. We can make a choice to act from a higher vibration of love, kindness and compassion instead. When we choose to hold space for joyful, creative, loving, non-reactionary energy, then we keep our own vibration levels in our energy body high and this in turn, brings the balance which we all seek, to love and thrive as our unique selves, yet very much aware of how we are one with the universe.

There is also a strong link between chakras two and four which can lead to an imbalance between both these energy centres especially when a person has been brought up to hide their affection and almost be expected to 'grow up' too soon without being allowed by parents and friends to have an open heart full of curiosity and feeling. In this type of scenario it is as if the restriction of showing feelings and emotions is squashed down between the second and the fourth chakras into the third chakra of ego identity and self-definition. An adult may show outward signs of great achievement and yet no amount of outward success at work and at sports, for example, will satisfy them because there is a disconnect with their true self that was shut down a long time ago. They feel an emptiness inside that no amount of material wealth can satisfy. Short term fixes from purchases may momentarily and artificially fill the gap but then the next morning or a week later, perhaps a month even, that emptiness has crept back into the psyche.

Moreover, they may find it difficult to hold down a long term relationship because they become bored easily and find difficulty in connecting with their inner child. Remember the importance of playfulness even as an adult! Perhaps you have known someone who was afraid of commitment or

who felt undeserving of finding love in a relationship? Maybe you know of a workaholic who thinks that they can channel all their energy into their work rather than taking time to relax and address their own emotional needs? These are all indicators of an imbalance with one's vulnerable and gentle heart chakra.

Furthermore, at this level it is not uncommon for a person to unconsciously adopt a pattern of loving that incurs an artificial pleasing of others in return for the perceived love that they think that they need or want in return. These behaviour patterns often change with increased maturity and life experience in later years as the sixth chakra is opened.

In chapter eight, when the sixth chakra is discussed, this chakra development is supported by the creativity and communication qualities of the fifth chakra. The developmental age when chakra six is heavily influenced is when a person becomes an adolescent or teenager and their mind is opened to increased possibilities of what the world can offer them, limited only by their imagination.

So what else can be done to heal and restore balance to this fourth chakra?

Suggested Affirmations to support balance in the fourth chakra are:

I give myself space to surrender to my own true feelings.

I am deeply loved and my presence on earth has been uniquely created for me.

I take care of myself with loving kindness and give myself downtime to rejuvenate and refresh my heart connection with the universe.

I celebrate the infinite abundance of love in all its forms and interact with others in a gentle loving and compassionate way.

I give intention to listen in love to my heart and to feel with my eyes.

I trust myself to know how to live and love.

I love myself enough to be still and allow my soul's wisdom to rise within me.

The beauty of a balanced fourth chakra is that the experiences and events that you create in your own reality broadcast joy, gratitude, love, kindness and appreciation.

There has never before been a more important time on this planet for us to generate our own individual time lines. What do I mean by this? Essentially, we each are the creators of our own awesome lives. When we are crystal clear on our intention of the life we want to manifest for ourselves then we can choose to raise our vibrational frequency beyond the linear world of duality and dullness and with a song, a smile, a dance, a walk in nature, a meditation or perhaps even laughter among friends and family, we start to resonate with the divine intelligence that is all around us and love life! These playful and joyous activities raise our consciousness to a higher level where we can live a higher dimensional life with ease and grace.

"

You can manifest what you want
when you don't give up too soon.
~ Molly McCord

Isn't this an awesome quote? Never quit on your dreams. Feel the love within you and the invisible energies around you that continually support you in love to help give you the strength and perseverance to follow what brings you passion in life. Remember it is a gift for you to ask for more light energy to come into your body to sustain your high energy and good health.

"

Can you allow peace to illuminate your road ahead
Settling in under the covers feeling safe and
protected every time you go to bed?
At the heart of your life you have absolute power
To experience love and flourish like a flower
Let go all the sadness, disillusionment and fear
Celebrate and rediscover the pleasures of life that
you create for yourself this year!
~ Lady Wise

CHAPTER 7

Chakra 5
Clarity of Communication

"

As your love grows along your enlightened pathway
Feel strengthened by your cosmic connection
with each passing day
When you speak and are heard in this expressive
chakra of sound vibration
This talent for speech will assist you in
powerful mediation!
~ Lady Wise

Having nourished, healed and balanced our body in the first four chakras with an acceptance and feeling of deep love and inner peace inside our heart, we can now turn our attention to the fifth chakra whose Sanscrit name is Vissudha meaning purification. Now we are entering the realms of sound, vibrations, creativity and communication, learning how we can speak and hear the truth. These expressions of self are how we flow with the rhythm of life! It is how we balance

the bridge between our inner world and the outer world. Our body is affected by every thought, word and action that we have, speak and do. Every cell in our cellular structure (and there are trillions of cells) vibrates as one with the others.

Did you know that based on co-creating our thoughts and emotions it is now possible to measure the frequency of our thoughts pioneered by Dr. Bruce H. Lipton (an internationally renowned leader in bridging science and spirit) using magnetoencephalography?

The quality of these vibrations establishes the building blocks of communication and our consciousness. Our feeling of connection is deepened with gratitude and heart coherence through a metaphysical core belief of love and the creative source within us.

"

There is more than meets the eye to absolutely every aspect and attribute of life itself.
~ Kryon

You can choose this opportunity to accelerate your intuition, your Higher Self, your inner connectedness with the universe (that was not known about even 50 years ago) in this new energy. You are able to create your life in prefect love using the synchronicities of the universe and the potentials available for your highest good when you establish two-way communication with the universe. This is doable in this new energy.

Every one of us is a piece of the creator source. We are one with the creator. We are all connected. In this way, we have the right to ask for enhanced intuition to support us in our daily life.

There is an enablement happening here that is different from anything, anytime ever on this planet. This is new.
~ Kryon

Each of us has the challenge of working through an old paradigm through an amazing journey into the new paradigm which allows us to see ourselves differently from what we were taught. Perception is everything.

We are presently the only generation accomplishing this quest while the Shift takes place on our watch. The children who have been born after 2012 have come in with a completely different perception about who they are, one that is more liberating because they are not confined to old beliefs that 'trap' human beings into thinking that they are victims of their world struggling with a purpose in life. For those Old Souls who have already had the breakthrough to higher thinking and for those who will to come, there is a greater maturity of understanding and knowingness that we are all part of an enlightened planet, the analogy for which Kryon refers to as the enlightened clock.

There will be some of the most compassionate, beautiful people on the planet and you will lose them. And through the sorrow of your heart you will implore God and say 'Why?' This was working. This person was beautiful, helping the planet, helping others. What happened? ...at some level you know the one that passed over is coming back soon to be grander than they ever were

Kryon explains this as the metaphor of the enlightened clocks where we each play our part in the wholeness of the evolution of humanity and keep 'ticking' even when we are feeling sorrow deep inside our hearts. We are all part of something so grand and elegant in this age of compassion.

I like to use the following phrase to keep me 'ticking' and inspiring others:-

"

*Right time, right place
With ease and grace!*

When you leave you will be with those who passed early. They may be your teachers, they may be your partners, but you will find them. This is part of the Old Soul's understanding of how things work. Presently, it is a small group that understands the age of compassion but this will become a much bigger group who innately know about the puzzle of life. We are slowly, one by one, 'awakening' to the truth that there is purpose in all we do. Human nature is positively changing.

It is about an individual consciousness of compassion and care for other human beings with integrity. The essence of peace on earth has its maturity in the paradigm of caring and understanding why things happen as they do.

Human nature is slowly changing and questioning through introspection who we are really. Humanity is challenging everything that is not operating with integrity, correctness and appropriateness as it covers everything from business systems, economics to politics and social systems. Kryon explains that there is going to be a revelation and a revolution in the energy of consciousness.

*We're going to be able to start doing things
by thinking about them.*
~ Kryon

Remember that the hardest part is often for us to imagine what is not already here. When I was younger I used to be and still am a keen photographer. I still have my Brownie camera received by me as a precious gift from my Papa. It was my first camera and I used it with black and white camera film. Mum, Dad and I travelled through to the old Forth Road Bridge, near Edinburgh so that I could take my first photographs of this magnificent structure. What has happened to camera film and to the whole chemical industry that virtually disappeared with it as recent as 2012? Without realising it things are changing. Change is constant. EVERYTHING IS POSSIBLE!

Perhaps it may not be long before batteries are no longer needed! This is already one of the potentials which is in the Field about which Kryon speaks. Instead, the power will be produced in a micro fashion by magnetics without the need for a grid and for batteries. Just think of the saving to the environment from dumping batteries once this is fully functional! It is already under development. Everything is polarised by the two elements positive and negative. This is a hint as to how such a development will be made. The

physics of today that is taught in education is incomplete. We are working with four laws of physics and we require to work with six laws of physics in order to create magnificent new inventions for our world here on planet earth.

I love listening to Kryon not just for teaching but to hear about the potentials of what are coming. Take gravity for example. Given that I have just told you that all energy has polarity, so too, therefore, does gravity. How else would you expect UFO aircrafts manage to fly away from planet earth? Ha! Are you prepared to think beyond what we currently have? Each law in physics which we have presently has two aspects – a push and a pull; a strong and a weak force. All that we need to work out is variable mass. The natural counterpoint that physics understands within the laws of physics is that there is always a 'push' to every 'pull'. Kryon explains that the UFOs have a variable mass lever. Our esoteric parents, the Pleiadians, are so much more advanced in their thinking that they have already worked out both polarities to gravity. How simple! This is a great reminder that there is nothing difficult. We either know how to do something or not.

There is so much more to our physical existence than we were ever told. There is no right or wrong way to learn more. Love and compassion are accelerators to this process. When you can stand strong and feel confident speaking your truth no matter what circumstances in which you find yourself, you will be guided through even the most challenging of situations by your entourage of guides, ancestors and other beautiful loving energies. Recently we have seen this vocal power exerted with the 'Black Lives Matter' campaign worldwide. Your voice is the liberating current of energy that flows through you and enhances your creativity to

flourish in all its magnificent forms. There are no two humans the same, not even twins.

How would you recognise if this current of creativity was being inhibited in you, due to the influence of other people? There are many indicators of trauma and abuse which may give rise to an energy blockage in this fifth chakra a few of which are mentioned as follows:-

When you are susceptible to someone who is very verbally abusive (often due to alcohol intake or other substance abuse) to you directly, and you allow this pattern to repeat especially when they are your partner, close friend or family member without saying anything;

When you feel afraid of telling the truth about a situation because you have been verbally threatened by the other party that your own life/safety may be in jeopardy if you dare to tell the truth to a third party;

When your partner, close friend, work colleague or family member, for example, tells you lies and you have third party evidence that confirms a different story (that of truth) yet you choose not to confront them;

Perhaps you were brought up in a strict family environment where you were discouraged from sharing your news from school or your joy about a new creative project in which you were involved. In many families, children can be treated by parents as 'objects' and there is no parental desire to listen to the children and so they are given money to 'disappear' for an hour, when the reality of that child is that they want to talk and have their feelings expressed and heard by the very parents whom they hold in regard;

A blatant and consistent show of material gifts and possessions bought for a child by its parents is symptomatic of a lack of interest and inability to listen by them (and indeed, also of an individual who, unable to express feelings, will assume that they can temporarily 'buy' the love and attention of their partner with material gifts in the short term to fill a gap in their own communication skills);

When your partner, close friend, work colleague or family member, for example, is constantly bullying you, intimidating you and shouting at you;

Children often grow up shy and introverted when their parents have repeatedly discouraged any comments spoken by the child and this has been further emphasised with such expressions to the child as, "Don't be so stupid!" or "Who do you think you are to have such dreams? They're not for people like us." These parental comments often transpire for several reasons:-

The parents do not have the knowledge to respond to the child's questions and do not want to appear as stupid themselves for not knowing;

The parents are projecting their own limiting thoughts and beliefs on to the child about what is and is not possible;

The parents are jealous of the child's creative abilities which are starting to show and seek to instantly quash them.

None of these reasons is healthy for either the parents or the child.

Sadly, when these examples materialise for a child as well as an adult, the child may grow up carrying these imbalances and often feeling guilty because they have been made to feel it is their fault, when it is not. The outcome of such trauma, however, may result in a deficiency in this chakra due to a perceived inability to speak up. An individual may have a very soft, quiet voice almost as if they are afraid to let anyone else hear their words. Sometimes too, a lack of vocabulary and/or an inability to express one's innermost feelings can occur because that person has not been used to receiving the nourishment and encouragement of speaking their own truth in an open and safe environment. Disappointingly, some children are born to those parents who either do not know how or who choose not to give their children much needed time to listen to that child's needs, feelings and thoughts. When a child is unable to freely express their feelings, the fifth chakra will start to close and effectively become toxic, hence the name Vissudha meaning purification of this particular chakra which must have the life source energy freely flowing through it of truth, self-expression and creativity to optimise its balance. Similarly, dysfunctions of the throat, neck and ears may physically manifest when there is either a deficiency or an excess specific to the fifth chakra.

It is not often I would ever ask you to think logically, ha! ha! but if a child or adult is consistently not being listened to and/or is having to tolerate yelling and examples of speech which are demeaning, abusive, authoritarian, lacking in dignity and disrespectful (to name just a few examples), then why would it be a surprise that deafness may become a problem? In this instance, the person does not want to hear what is going on in their outer world when the words that they hear are consistently derogatory and lacking in both love and compassion. Unfortunately what may happen over time is that the person on the receiving end effectively tunes out to every conversation and this shuts down their flow of consciousness as well. Can you understand this? What is especially sad in this scenario is that the person delivering the abusive words does not realise that every time they utter such words, they are adversely impacting their own energy levels and encouraging a pattern of negativity that vibrates throughout their own chakra system too. Remember that our cellular structure cannot differentiate when we are talking to ourselves and when we are talking to or about another person(s). Our cellular structure hears the words and assumes they are all for the Self. This means that anyone who talks in a negative way, including gossiping, is self-sabotaging their own magnificence. This is done in ignorance, which is why I am passionate about giving you the opportunity to become more empowered so that you can choose for yourself your own sacred, abundant path in celebration of your own magnificence, unique talents and gifts.

When the fifth chakra is out of balance the reason may be due to:-

- a deficiency;

- an excess in that chakra or

- a combination of both a deficiency reason and an excess reason.

How many times have you heard an individual state they have a fear of public speaking? This is a deficiency of the fifth chakra. Similarly when one has a very weak voice and/ or struggles to be able to express themselves through their words, this suggests a deficiency also. It may be because that person feels that to speak out would result in them being made fun of, criticised or perhaps rejected by their peers and/or family members and friends. Anxiety and tensions may be compounded when the individual struggles to make their needs heard and builds up frustration at their inability to communicate what and how they feel. In addition, it is not uncommon for shyness to be an attribute of a deficient fifth chakra. This characteristic suggests a person who is lacking in self-confidence and very sensitive to how others respond to them when they do and do not speak. Often a child who has been forbidden to speak as a child can exude shyness in adolescence and into their adult years. There is a need to bolster that person's self-respect and to reassure them that they are worthy of expressing their emotions and their point of view. The likelihood is that an introverted person would also have a deficient fifth chakra because this attribute once again is challenging the human being's right to assert themselves as autonomous, take charge of their life and trust themselves to stay strong and speak their truth without fear of recrimination. In an extreme case, the person will be hindered from both an ability to express themselves and further to absorb new information. They can become completely blocked.

How good are you at dancing to the rhythm of a drum or your favourite song? What is your favourite music to listen to? Music is wonderful for shaking up our energy. The fifth chakra expands our life force connection with our vibration of movement and the energy that flows within us to allow us to express our individual creativity in all its forms. The extent to which we can resonate with situations, circumstances and people in the world around us will determine our health and vitality within our body and mind. A quote from one of the greatest scientists, Nikola Tesla, for whom I have great admiration is:-

If you want to find the secrets of the universe,
think in terms of energy, frequency and vibration.

When we are unable to flow with the rhythm of life and literally have poor rhythm this is also symptomatic of a deficient fifth chakra. Each of us needs to be able to live our truth as an original creator. We are here on earth to create, create, create. Communication is the creative expression of all that is within us supported by the two-way connection of our soul and the creative source of all that is in the outer world.

Remember though that each chakra may also be operating in excess from scenarios which have created an imbalance. One of my friends recently commented on a new employee who was very personable but who simply never stopped talking. This individual was discharging the energy that was building up through their throat chakra to relieve stress. It created much frustration from the manager in the early days because she was reluctant to pass comment to the new start given her enthusiasm for work. Once she realised the reason for this excessive behaviour, however, she was able to calmly nurture the employee to channel her energy into her hobby of singing which helped to heal this excess in the fifth chakra. The healing practice of singing allowed the person to work with her voice in a different way. Over two months the employee's singing improved greatly and furthermore, her confidence in her day job dramatically improved for the better to the extent that she was more assertive while not feeling the need to talk as much, unless the matter was of relevance to her work environment. Can you understand how the healing benefitted everyone with whom this individual came into contact?

When one person starts to focus their energies within and raise their vibration, this energy shift is not only seen by others in a positive way but it positively impacts on the energy field of others around them too at both conscious and unconscious levels.

Another potential sign of an excessive fifth chakra is when an individual consistently talks as a defence about their thoughts, words and actions. They may be particularly exaggerated in their arguments to preserve their position of power. This is merely a way for that person to stay in control which may be symptomatic of displaced anger and frustration, but also a resistance by that individual to feel into their body and have confidence to speak their truth about meaningful situations and their true underlying feelings instead of occupying their consciousness with gobbledegook or nonsense that has no real substance to its content. Deep down this individual may fiercely protect their vulnerabilities and go to great lengths to avoid and hide them feeling insecure and mistrusting of humanity, while to the outside world they will be revered and viewed as exceptional communicators.

Under this element of sound, the significance of a balanced fifth chakra extends to the tone, clarity and rhythm of one's voice. Someone who is always keen to interrupt a conversation and insists on being the loudest party in a group, overpowering others decisions and opinions without regard for those which are different from their own, is indicative of an excess fifth chakra condition.

The balance of the fifth chakra is as dependent on an individual becoming a good creator and communicator as well as a good listener. A further example of an excessive fifth chakra would include a person who has a strong inability

to listen. I am sure you all have stories of this type of person with whom you have encountered on your own life's journey to date, but since gossiping is also an attribute of an excess then let's leave it right here. Ha! One final excess characteristic which is linked to hearing is that of poor auditory comprehension. I remember well my poor French aural comprehension marks in secondary three at school when, despite my best efforts, I would frequently achieve an average mark of only two and a half points out of a maximum of twenty. Indeed, the whole class generally attained exceptionally low marks for this subject too and we always blamed it on the French teacher who had been dux of her class when younger but disappointingly struggled to impart her knowledge. Perhaps it was a combination of both factors!

What I find especially interesting is that in order to be an excellent communicator one also has to be a very good listener. And yes, I am sure this is indeed why humans are born with two ears and only one mouth! Ha! Seriously though, the art of communication rests in our ability to both stop and listen to our inner voice of calm, creativity and wisdom as well as being able to be a good listener in our outer world with one another and with nature. The self-assurance must come from knowing deep in your heart that truly all that you have experienced to date has been necessary for your life lessons and that there is no right or wrong path that you may have taken in the past. Everything that has brought you to this point today has purpose.

It is possible to have a fifth chakra in which one aspect of imbalance is deficient and another is excessive within this same chakra. For example, an individual may be an excellent communicator at their office as the Chief Executive Officer full of bravado, charisma and aplomb, but when they go home they are very reserved and unable to express their intimate thoughts and feelings to their loved one.

Our invisible Merkaba or 8 metre field that is around our corporeal body holds all the information from our past lifetimes and sometimes old traumas can be blocking our energies and contributing to an imbalanced chakra. This is another reason why it is important to drop your karma because in this new energy it is no longer serving you and is an added hindrance to your well-being. This is very easily done. Simply decide in pure love that this is the right decision for you and when you are ready take a quiet moment in stillness without interruption or disruption around you, take a couple of deep breaths imagining inhaling beauty and exhaling negativity and all toxins, you are now ready to commit to dropping your karma forever with the following words, "I drop my karma and move on."

I want to emphasise that everything is connected and some things are more connected than others. The fifth chakra includes the creation of one's thoughts and words using one's voice and works directly with the second chakra related to expressing the sexual, sensual aspects of creation in manifesting physical pleasure and matter. Any anxieties or worries about one's sex life, for example, may cause a problem in the throat area, when that person feels unable and uncomfortable to freely speak openly and express their truth about these feelings to their partner/loved-one.

So what can be done to heal and restore balance to this fifth chakra?

There are various healing modalities for restoring good health to this chakra of self-expression.

Journal writing can be very beneficial to unlock creative talent that does not necessarily need to be shown to anyone else, yet tackles the allowance of natural flow of creative expression through thoughts and words. There is a freedom in being able to write absolutely anything without worrying about typos, grammar, the scale of individual letter sizes and ink colour. For someone who has been deficient and lacked confidence in finding the right words to express their feelings this form of healing is a wonderful private and therapeutic solution to enable the individual to feel inspired and increasingly confident about who they are. Equally, journal writing may be a perfect past time for that person who was always so talkative, but who now prefers to write down their thoughts and feelings without feeling guilty about provoking others with their incessant rants and spoken verbiage.

Automatic writing is another form of healing to balance the fifth chakra for which all you need is a piece of paper and a pen. May I suggest you create your own little zone of calm preferably at a table where you can sit with your feet flat on the ground with the paper and pen in front of you on the table laid out in any way you like. Always remember there is no right or wrong way, there is only your way. I am merely giving you a few suggestions to get started (which you may choose to change too!). Place the palms of your hands facing down on the table gently relaxed and closing your eyes take a couple of deep nourishing breaths into your heart centre to settle you down and bring you more into the present moment. Your feet flat on the floor will help to ground you. Next, take the pen in your normal writing hand and simply allow any thoughts that you have to flow on to the paper. Just allow the pen to move and go with the flow! There is no need to look at what you are writing until you feel that it is time to stop. Once you have sensed that everything has been put down, take a look and attempt to make sense of it. This can be as much fun as the automatic writing itself as you juggle the paper at different angles to determine what you have written. I would suggest that you look not just for words but also symbols too. This is a lovely way to connect with your heart, brain, pineal gland and the divine spark of creation that is within you as it connects to the divine spark of the universe outside of you. It is a great introduction to encouraging you to work with your quantum abilities rather you're your logical capabilities. Spirit cannot connect with us in a linear way because it exists in quantum realms and so symbols are often a 'bridge' in communicating with us. Magical!

The art of storytelling either verbally or in writing is a great technique for helping someone to balance their fifth chakra. An acquaintance I met many years ago at the Edinburgh Festival had a penchant for storytelling and writing poetry as a wonderful way to relax and chill out from her day job as a nurse. This activity can also be used as a method for describing different role play characters that may mirror the issues of the individual who has not been allowed to speak their truth in their own reality or when an attempt has been made to do so they have been ridiculed or rejected by others. The opportunity to express this frustration through story telling gives the author back their voice to act out the scenario in different ways with different outcomes.

Very often most of us become stuck in a linear world of goal setting and target achievement. I totally understand how goals can be an incentivising benchmark to propel us forward and to make progress. They can also, however, be the scourge of our existence and drive us so hard to the end game that

we never enjoy the journey to get there, we lose all sensitivity and awareness which is what our life is all about and when we reach our goal the satisfaction is short term because we feel unsettled again with who we are and think that setting more goals to achieve is the solution. Whereas when there is total balance throughout one's body and an understanding of that something that is bigger than us (creator source of all that is), then we gravitate to an inner knowingness that relaxes all need for goals in our life. We start to live our life moment to moment with a connectedness that enables us to let go and go with the flow! This may sound, for want of a better expression, foolish, but the essence of this inner peace and confidence comes from a wisdom that is higher thinking. The ego is let go and as we trust in the universe for all that we desire, all that we desire is added to our lives in divine time. Remember you are known by spirit, the creator source, God or by another name as appropriate to your beliefs. Therefore, in every moment so too is your every thought, desire and dream known by the same source without you having to utter one word. It all ties back to that link to the consciousness of everything. When you trust, trust, trust, trust, trust in this, then all you have to do is know in your heart that when the time is right for you these things will manifest. There is no need to worry which leaves a whole lot of extra time for you to live your sacred joy! There is no need to be scared of life. Did you notice that scared uses the same letters as the word sacred only in a different order? Let me remind you that love and fear cannot co-exist. When you choose to live a life of sustained joy filled with love and laughter, no feelings of fear or being scared can exist. You choose how you feel in every nano-second. Feel free to set yourself some goals but from the knowingness that the creator source knows who you are and will gift these to you at the right time in the right place. It is by having an open heart ready to receive that these goals will manifest and not by the ego driven force of sheer effort.

All that is great always comes as a gift.
Don't strive for it, otherwise you will miss.
~ Osho

The healing practice of involving yourself in a non-goal oriented creative activity can help to balance the fifth chakra in this case. As an example, restoring one's health may be considerably helped by taking a walk in nature and selecting some leaves to create a random picture once you have returned home. Alternatively the leaves can be used as a silhouette to a backdrop colour collage, delicately pressed in a book or simply positioned on a window sill and admired for their natural beauty. May I suggest you take your inspiration from nature and feel what you are inspired to do next?

The body has a natural resonance with all of its cells acting as one and also with the vibrational frequency of the outer world in which we live. The invisible 8 metre Merkaba which is around every human being, shifts and changes constantly with our own feelings, emotions and thoughts. Part of this Merkaba contains our aura which can be viewed using Kirlian photography. I was able to witness the responses to the subtle vibrations of our thoughts and related activity on the aura when I observed a friend's aura both before reiki and then during and after a reiki treatment. As I was applying reiki to her, the colours in her auric field were changing and rising in colour way up the chakra

colour spectrum. Our ability to influence our body's energy flow is subtle. The throat is the narrowest passage within the whole chakra system and so if this is blocked then we are not able to allow the natural flow of energy up into the sixth and seventh chakras, nor can we receive the downward energy into our first chakra to manifest those intuitive thoughts that are incoming to our inner self. The neck becomes very important in this process. A stiff neck and shoulder area may build up due to the stress of a person unable to speak what they know. The corollary of this would be when a person may be very prone to doing things on a whim without the understanding and awareness of the new information that the free flowing energy of the seventh chakra brings to the issue. Perhaps a gentle shoulder and neck massage would help the release of tension in this area. I remember choosing a champissage treatment over a foot massage at a girls party night years ago and it was absolutely amazing. I felt the benefits from such a relaxing treatment for several days thereafter.

Given that the art of communication and creativity is the purpose of a balanced fifth chakra, work done on one's voice will be very healing and balancing. The extent to which the voice is clear, concise in its expression and speaks truthfully will determine a resonant and rhythmic voice in balance.

Without realising it, our voice denotes the health of the fifth chakra and other chakras as well. If there is a lack of balance in these other chakras then the indicators of this in the voice may include the following:-

Chakra 1: Without the right to exist and be here, the physical body may feel restricted in some way and contract the voice;

Chakra 2: Without a person able to feel their responses to the outside world, the voice may sound hostile, matter of fact or mechanical;

Chakra 3: When the voice sounds very weak and peevish, this high-pitched sound indicates a deficient third chakra;

Alternatively, when the voice sounds very dominating and loud this suggests an excessive third chakra;

Chakra 4: Without breath the voice would not function and so an uneven or potentially stifled voice that is short on breath and lacking in full rhythm indicates an imbalance in the fourth chakra;

Chakra 6: When an individual is shut off from their intuition and lives in their logical mind of duality, their voice will become very dull and boring to listen to;

Chakra 7: Without an understanding, knowledge or genuine interest in the topic spoken, the voice will come across monotone without any vitality or expression.

Each chakra has its own mantra sound which is used to encourage all sound to come through one's body, more effectively than without the exercise.

One of my yoga teachers from over twenty years ago, Yogi Nirmalendu, used to encourage us to use sound by way of a chant, "Sho-Hum" whenever we felt a little anxious or worried about something. The result of this was to recalibrate our basic vibrational essence. Out with a particular need, we would spend about fifteen minutes in his yoga class quietly sitting and chanting this in a low, controlled volume. It was very relaxing, calming and rhythmic. I was especially thrilled to participate in this part of the class because I love any kind of singing!

When I was out in Australia several years ago I was introduced to a lady who practices Sound Therapy as one healing modality. There is a variety of tools that can be used to assist in sound healing such as Tibetan singing bowls, drums and tuning forks. I have chosen to focus the balance exercises using only the voice as an instrument and referring to three methods:-

1. Seed sounds sourced from ancient tantric texts used to help restore healing and rejuvenate the chakras;

2. Vowel sounds associated with each chakra;

3. Tuning forks aligned to each chakra in the chakra system of seven.

These methods will provide the best outcomes when they are consistently used and repeated over a period of time.

The voice has an ability to resonate sound with those vowels which have a specific meaning to the part of the body to which they refer and to affect our innermost being. By simply focusing on one particular sound and chanting this, it can actively help to release blockages in the part of the body to which that sound relates. Mantras are chants which are uttered silently in the mind. It is up to you to decide whether you would prefer to chant these seed and/or vowel sounds aloud or to silently chant them as a mantra. When you are chanting the sounds aloud, let the sound come out as naturally as possible and adjust your body stance as you feel appropriate to allow the pulsating energy to flow. You may choose to do this by yourself or as part of a group.

The seed sounds for each chakra are as follows:-

Chakra One: Seed sound LAM

Chakra Two: Seed sound VAM

Chakra Three: Seed sound RAM

Chakra Four: Seed sound YAM

Chakra Five: Seed sound HAM

Chakra Six: Seed sound OM

No seed sound is given for Chakra Seven because this seventh chakra is transcending time and space. It is one with the cosmic consciousness realm of creator source, God, spirit. It is quantum in its connection.

The vowel sounds for each chakra are as follows:-

Chakra One: Vowel sound 'Ohh' (as in toad)

Chakra Two: Vowel sound 'Oooo' (as in stool)

Chakra Three: Vowel sound 'Ahh' (as in car)

Chakra Four: Vowel sound 'Ayy' (as in play)

Chakra Five: Vowel sound 'Eeee' (as in sleep)

Chakra Six: Resonant sound 'Mmm'

Chakra Seven: Resonant sound 'Nngg'

In Tibetan numerology the number nine means completion. May I suggest that you chant these sounds for nine seconds at a time, break for nine seconds and then repeat the

chanting practice for a further nine seconds, rest for nine seconds and do this for a third time. The intermission between each chant for nine seconds gives you time to reflect and feel the resonance of your chanting sound throughout your being. After you have finished this see how you feel about your breath and about the quality of sound that you created coupled with how your body feels specific to the parts of the body for which this particular sound is the focus. Remember that these sounds are expected to stimulate the elemental qualities of these chakras and the body parts to which they refer. Be open to the feelings and vibrations that resonate throughout your body as you do this. Make it fun! When you are feeling more confident you can make up your own chants/ mantras by linking in other chanting sounds from other chakras as part of a larger exercise and lengthen the time for chanting and resting accordingly.

Have you heard of the beautiful Solfeggio frequencies and tones? The sacred solfeggio scale represents musical notes that have a designated frequency in Hz (Hertz), that resonate and vibrate to nature, the earth and to the chakras in our bodies to finely tune them to purity and healing perfection in a 'number' of ways.

The electro-magnetic frequencies of these tones have been used in the Gregorian Chants and have been forgotten by most souls until recently. Each tonal frequency that we listen to helps us to heal in a different way. Even when you are healthy and free from any ailments these are the perfect sounds to listen to in order to maintain a healthy and balanced system. I find them so relaxing and comforting that I often fall asleep to them.

174 Hz creates a foundation for the acceleration and evolution of consciousness. According to some sources, this tone can provide your body with a sense of security, safety and love, reducing pain energetically. Pain can be hugely debilitating to one's wellbeing in the same way that pain relief can be a huge contributor to one's wellbeing. The purpose of the first chakra is to create a strong foundation for our body to support the spiritual flow of life force energy which gives us life and to support our spiritual right to connect with our divine spark within in whatever way we consider appropriate.

258 Hz tones send a message to the body to restructure the damaged organs of the body by sending messages to the tissues which bring them to their original form. It is particularly healing for burns and fractures.

396 Hz has a function of assisting any grief felt by the person listening to the frequency to be converted into joy! How remarkable and benevolent is that? This frequency can also help with the release of fear and guilt. Remembering that love and fear cannot co-exist and that the way to greater spiritual understanding and wholeness is through the heart and self-love. When we learn how to fall in love with ourselves we trigger a rejuvenation of our life force energy. Moreover, you may well surprise yourself when you have no self-doubt and are oozing with confidence!

417 Hz when listened to is wonderful for facilitating change and cleansing the energy field from any traumatic circumstances and situations. When the will is strong in the third chakra and we have balanced the first two chakras of grounding (earth) and of feeling and emotion (water), we are able to willingly participate in the changes that we need to enrich our lives and to grow.

528 Hz is referred to by some individuals as the Miracle Tone and I would associate this frequency primarily with the fourth heart chakra. It is the natural frequency of Mother Earth, Gaia, Pachamama and repairs DNA. It is a wonderful tone to listen to as your DNA restores itself to balance. Furthermore, it brings about transformation and miracles into one's life. I am most certainly all for that. "I believe in miracles, I do, I do, I do!" This is the title of one of my unfinished manuscripts!

Among the first musicians to record in the third note of the ancient Solfeggio musical scale, which has also been called the 'LOVE frequency', were selective recordings of John Lennon and Sir Paul McCartney. These were performed in the 528Hz frequency. According to Dr. Leonard Horowitz's research, published on the Internet and in 'The Book of 528: Prosperity Key of LOVE', this particular frequency is associated with the "centre of the musical-mathematical matrix of creation" and recognised by many as "pure tone LOVE." He considered that the 'LOVE frequency' resonated at the heart of everything including nature. Mathematicians and physicists have now proven 528 vibrates at the heart of the universe, rainbows, God's heart and yours. It will be no surprise to you, therefore, to know that more and more artists in recent years have chosen to record in this uplifting frequency such as Dolly Parton, Celine Dion, Eric Clapton, Foreigner, Sting and Ameriie.

Listening in love whether it is to music, our own heart-beat, or to our own voice restores a sense of wholeness of who we are and what our purpose is on planet earth. Know that every choice you make affects your vibration. Choose high vibration and coherence of your heart! It is in this heart coherence that we appreciate the balance of our life in relation to ourselves as an individual and to others. This is the trigger for love and compassion. The link between the seventh chakra and the fourth chakra is the understanding and wisdom that comes from the seventh chakra as it feeds the fourth chakra's purpose of love and balance. Change is constant but when we have built in ourselves a solid core of inner peace and calmness, we are able to tackle all joy and adversity that comes our way. Furthermore, since you will come to realise through your own sacred journey of self-discovery (do not take my word for it) that you are your own creator and there is no such thing as chance, you can ensure that all your life is blessed with ease and grace!

638 Hz governs the throat chakra or fifth chakra and enhances communication, creativity and general understanding. Moreover, it enhances talents and love and is particularly appropriate for strengthening relationships.

741 Hz is appropriate for enhancing the power of self-expression which results in a pure and stable life and furthermore, assists in clearing the physical cells of all toxins. The benefits from listening to this frequency oriented to self-expression are also synonymous with the fifth chakra.

852 Hz helps to awaken intuition and returns vibration to spiritual order. The sixth chakra whose Sanscrit name is Ajna (to perceive) will be assisted by this sound to further improve one's imagination, psychic perception and to discern clarity on the interpretation of dreams, symbols and fantasies enabling us to open up to a new realm of possibilities. Indeed, the development of the sixth chakra is often referred to as spiritual awakening.

963 Hz restores one's spirit to original settings and is directly connected to light. This frequency is excellent for opening

the pineal gland. It is the triad of the heart, the brain and the pineal gland which works together with the divine spark, our soul, which is within us, which connects to the universal soul of creator source, God, spirit. Remember that this journey of our soul on the path of light is one that restores our wholeness and capabilities that we have always had, which were 'hidden' from us until we decided with free choice to find out more about ourselves. This is the reason that self-love is the only way to access our wholeness and oneness.

Thankfully, sound frequency is being remembered by more and more souls as a healing tonic.

The purpose of toning is not only in the form of frequencies and music to be listened to which, if you remember, is a good characteristic of the fifth chakra. Toning is also a way of exercising one's voice. Using tones can provide many hours of pleasure working with both the body and the breath to literally just see what sounds come out! Ha! There is no structure required to force any words or sounds out of one's mouth. Whenever there are feelings and emotions flowing through our body there is a need for movement to be expressed. If such fluidity is repressed or suppressed then blockages in the chakra can occur.

How about taking fifteen minutes to find enough standing room to stand with your feet shoulder width apart and allowing your arms to gently fall by your sides? Without becoming embarrassed, lightly shake your body about a bit, flex your fingers open and closed, perhaps start to gently swing your arms or rotate them if you have enough space and allow any, grunts, groans, squeaks, barfs etc. to be expressed from your throat. The more relaxed you are the more you will naturally 'just be' with whatever you choose

to express. Such a release of tension and inertia will help you to clear any blockages in your fifth chakra.

The excessive fifth chakra exercise of practising a quietening of the mind and voice and through being silent is suggested. It may be easier for an individual to sit down in a place where they know they will not be disturbed for fifteen minutes and use the opportunity to stop and find the stillness within them. The ability to stop, sit in silence and listen is a method for receiving intuition. The person can use the pause from talking to sense, feel, hear and know. It is another way for allowing a heart coherence using the triad of the heart, brain and pineal gland to connect with the creator source and receive information from the universe such as intuition. Not all information comes from the brain. The brain is like a computer that is not the source of all information. It sometimes simply acts as the messenger and interpreter of the information from the creator source. Remember this is how most of the classic composers, Albert Einstein and Nikola Tesla sourced their inspiration. It comes from a central source that can only be reached when you are still and in a heart coherence filled with love, compassion and joy. It does not come from your mind!

How we use colour has a profound influence on our emotions and confidence. In the Western world especially, there still seems to be a general reluctance by people to embrace colours in their clothing, yet in the Eastern World there is a plethora of colour used in all things, particularly fabrics as a wonderful attribute of a creator's choice. On my visits to Bali, Singapore and Dubai the array of colours envisioned both in the variety of foodstuffs and textiles has been a real privilege to experience and such visits have been inspirational to me personally in initiating colour palettes that I put together in my own wardrobe. Presently, three of my favourite colour combinations are mango and turquoise as one set, passionflower red and royal purple as a second choice followed by the trio of gold, silver and copper. Remember what I mentioned about the link of the fifth chakra to the second chakra? The colour turquoise or bright blue is synonymous with the fifth chakra, while orange is identified as the second chakra colour. With a balanced second chakra we freely allow the sensate realm (sight, sound, touch, taste and smell) to respond with feeling to the incoming experiences from the outer world. These feelings give us our well-being through healthy sexuality and as a foundation for establishing what we want, whereas with a balanced fifth chakra we are expressing outwardly to the world what is inside of us with honesty and truth which has evolved and been influenced from the intake of experiences.

We can positively influence our own mood and that of those with whom we mingle and associate through the strength of colour. This usually takes place at a subliminal level but its impact is no less impactful for this and it frequently works in our favour. Allow me to give you an example. Many years ago I attended a day seminar about communication. Prior to this I decided to wear a turquoise top and black skirt to 'attract' like minded individuals who would resonate with my choice of colour. Sure enough, at the first intermission in the morning, this lady approached me and asked me if I was already aware of the power of colour and especially the colour turquoise governing the fifth chakra, that of communication. I laughed and replied that I was and a fascinating conversation ensued!

Together with other healing practices we can boost our own self-confidence and mood as an aid to overall balance

using colour in our clothing and accessories, jewellery and hair.

Suggested Affirmations to support balance in the fifth chakra are:

I am expressing truth, joy and love with my sexuality.

I am true to myself and assert my needs for my highest good.

I am always in the right place at the right time.

I am my own unique creator of my life.

I am self-assured and able to think for myself independently of others.

I am able to look within and listen to the inner voice of my heart in peace, truth and with clarity.

The sign of a healthy fifth chakra embodies our creativity as this energy travels onwards and upwards through the sixth chakra and up to the seventh chakra of understanding. In addition to acknowledging this upward, expansive energy which has its grounding in Mother Earth and is the energy stored in matter, we are able to receive inspiration by the downward energy as it flows from the seventh chakra towards the first chakra where we hold the power to manifest our ideas and thoughts discovered in the seventh chakra in harmony and with perfect communication to the outside world. There is no longer any awkwardness, shyness or constraints of regret in what is being inspired, created and communicated. Instead, there is a strong connection, a two-way communication of the individual who can express themselves with newly found empathy and compassionate communication to others, now that they are able to relate to and receive loving support and information from their Higher Self, God, spirit, creator source and the universe. Let your inspiration become the catalyst for your creativity!

"

The subtle world of sound and vibration
Has its roots in the source of all creation
Mastery and balance of this chakra's incongruity
Will inspire you with infinite possibilities of opportunity!
~ Lady Wise

CHAPTER 8

Chakra 6
Clear Vision

"

Rise up from the illusion of what you think you see
And focus on living clear and authentically
Avoidance of repetitive cycles will restore clarity of vision
Guiding you to positively deal with any
impending decision!
~ Lady Wise

This sixth chakra whose Sanscrit name is Ajna is all about being able to see patterns and having the understanding and knowledge to interpret these with clarity.

In a linear world, the majority of us have lead our lives unaware of negative repeat cycles that we live through because we are not thinking from a higher perspective and using our intuition to trigger an awareness of what is best for our highest good. Often, such divisive patterns originate from deep programming that transcends multiple lifetimes and time-lines. Now, in this lifetime, in this Shift of human

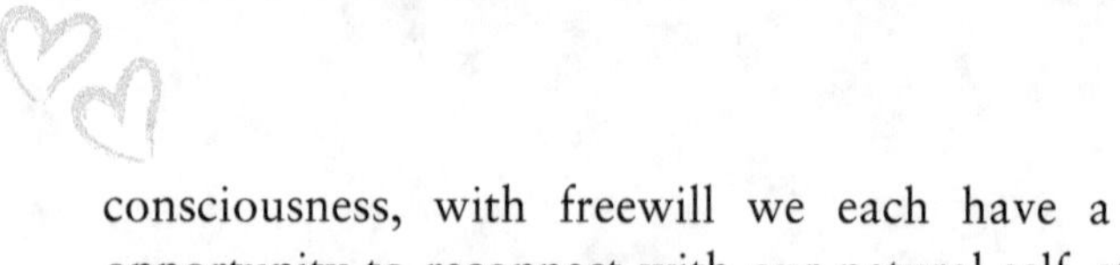

consciousness, with freewill we each have a fast-track opportunity to reconnect with our natural self, step up and take responsibility for what we need to do to make changes for a better, healthier, wholeness of life.

We are going through an upgrade of humanity on planet earth and this, in turn, is elevating the consciousness of Gaia and the whole Galaxy. Throughout this thirty-six year cycle of the Precession of the Equinoxes from 1994 to 2030, there is a wider acceleration of the breakdown and deconstruction of the old order. Have you noticed what is no longer working for humanity on the planet? Everything that has not been based on a strong foundation of truth, integrity and fairness is collapsing. This is causing a great deal of tension on the planet and especially within countries rather than between countries. When you understand the context of this in the bigger picture of shaping a new world for humanity based on freedom, trust and peace, then you have the choice to switch off media news and other gossip that is disturbing to your ears and inciting unfounded fear.

Instead, you have the maturity and understanding to recognise the drama playing out in duality for what it is, and to rise above this reality and shape your own reality of higher thinking and compassion, where you are in control of creating the life you want for yourself, regardless of what is going on in the outer world. THIS IS THE POWER OF YOU!

It's time to set a new intention for yourself and for humanity. When you live true to your own authentic self and feel the freedom to be creative and honest in all you do, natural health follows. It has to, because you are living in harmony and balance with your true self.

Are you remembering that everyday can be a day of learning and growing in knowledge and wisdom? Very often the teenage years are a time of realisation that there is a grand world to explore which captures our imagination and gently pushes us to increasingly question who we are in relation to it all. At this stage we often expand our ideas about our own personal identity and formulate different perspectives on how our taking up space in the world fits in to the larger vista. Indeed, this can be a lifelong questioning that occupies our mind for much of the time. Ha!

The balance of this sixth chakra for which the birthright 'to see' is the basic right, comes from an ability to connect strongly with one's inner feelings to determine whether the outward life that we have made for ourselves is a true projection of our real self.

Let me describe a scenario for you that may manifest when a person is out of sync with this chakra. They may be having hallucinations or bad dreams at night and find it difficult to concentrate. When a person has created a life for themselves that is built up on an outer world perception of what is expected of them to achieve, such as going to university, meeting a partner, securing a great job and living in a beautiful home with a family, but that person's own genuine inner spirit is to be an adventurer and travel the world independently without any family ties or corporate job commitments that would have them work more than twelve hours a day just to keep the business afloat, for example, then eventually the bubble bursts. Perhaps a divorce arises and the person loses their job at the corporate company because they can no longer concentrate on their job. Their own truth about who they are has to reveal itself eventually even when this takes years. Any imbalance or disconnect between a person's daily

life and their underlying true personal identity of who they believe themselves to be requires to be healed.

Effectively what this person has done is to create an image around what they imagined was what was expected of them rather than connecting deep within their heart to reveal the core truth of their authentic self. Their outer world ultimately has to implode because they are not living their truth. Sadly, this can often be a major shock to a person who may not understand why their whole outer world seems to be collapsing in on them and they feel powerless.

One of the principal causes of this disconnect with the true reality of who we are occurs when we immerse ourselves in television, drama, films, magazines, billboards and social media that has us artificially believing that what we visually observe is the ideal way of life with all its material assets, perceived 'perfect' model figures etc. These may contribute to us creating illusions in our mind that this is the ultimate goal in life without an understanding that much of what we see under these circumstances is delusional. It is as if we are going about our lives wearing rose-coloured spectacles oblivious to the core truth of the real reality that we are able to create for ourselves that honours and respects ourselves.

In essence, the opening of the third eye between our eyebrows allows us to see only our true self and not perceived images of what we think we want to be and become. How often have you heard the expression of William Shakespeare repeated?

"

The eyes are the gateways to the soul.

When the third eye is opened, we start to see with insight and the gift of intuition the patterns that our ego has had us follow, rather than the pursuit of a pattern that is for our highest good. It is as if a new light, the light of consciousness and connection to the universe, is imbued within us and allows us to observe the bigger existence in which we each have the choice to flourish.

"

The more conscious a person becomes, the more his choices will lead to happiness; the more unconscious he is, the closer he will move towards misery.
~ OSHO

No matter how much change is going on around you, you always have control over how you respond! Remember that change allows you to develop and grow and is for your highest good. It's time to understand the patterns of your ego mind that have been giving you a false sense of power. Once you can see the repeated patterns that have been occurring in your life, you are able to take a step back, metaphorically, and start to appreciate the wonders of what you are capable and of what is really in your heart. The energy of the new world requires you to drop the false ego and reconnect with how you feel in your heart.

In the past, even if you have been outstandingly successful (by whatever standards you rate your success) operating from an ego based program, this will no longer work in the new energy of love and compassion. There is already a reworking of one's ego at an invisible energetic level and this reprogramming, if you will, is at a deep level bringing in the balance of the divine feminine energies that have been pushed

out by the dominance of the divine male energies for eons. We are being encouraged to align with our spiritual power! This transformation or shift at the energetic level is providing us with amazing opportunities to heal all our fears and to feel what is the best choice for us to take next, from the higher perspective of trusting in our intuition and feeling what is right in our heart.

The biggest lesson for us to learn is to trust ourselves! When we learn to trust ourselves then we can take this out to all our other relationships. Sometimes the greatest fear for us can be to sit in calmness and in a space of protection and safety that allows us to listen to our intuition. This is a deep ask but it is a very worthwhile ask because when you explore the darkness of your soul you realise that there has always been a spark of light within you that is eager to show you a deeper way to trust yourself and to help you create even bigger dreams for yourself than you could ever have imagined. This light within you is like an eternal flame of hope, love, safety, protection and creativity. It waits for you to understand more of your inner world before it shows itself to you. When you can trust yourself and feel supported by this very intuitive energy within you, you will feel like you have taken off a heavy overcoat of fears, drama and emotionally charged negative experiences all at once to reveal a beautiful being of light, love and happiness. This is who you are!

There is no need to pander to the external drama of the day when you can come fully alive with your internal world of imagination, creativity and feel fear free! You have always travelled with wisdom inside of you but until you choose to transform beyond the linear life of your ego and follow your heart, such a higher vibrational energy is not made available to you.

Listen to the messages from your heart
Reclaim your inner wisdom that is yours to impart
Feel encouraged by what you trust is to come
Remember to smile and connect in peace with everyone!
~ Lady Wise

As with each of the chakras discussed, we are essentially moving forward in our journey of wholeness. The balancing of the sixth chakra requires you to let go all logical thought and to trust in your intuition. It is from your intuition that you receive a clarity and strength on which you can always depend to give you those internal whispers for your highest good.

"

Everything can change in the twinkle of an eye
But a trusting heart will guide you, when all else
seems awry
Regardless of strange happenings, this is
no time to be bored
Awaken your senses to new ways to be explored!
~ Lady Wise

The Ajna vision is the gift to be able to see things in a different way. This may be specifically for your own benefit or it may extend to a grander project involving hundreds of people and the introduction of innovative creations that offer an awesome benefit to many.

We are all in a massive galactic shift of exciting energetic vibrations that are breaking down the individual ego of 'me' and necessitating the higher thought of 'we' in relation to a

more expansive creative world of unifying everyone. This brings a whole new challenge to the word 'team'. Ha! For years many have spoken in corporate seminars that there is no 'I' in 'team'. There is of course the word 'me' hidden in 'team' and so perhaps we need a brand new expansive word to describe a group of people working or playing together? Remember we are all multi-dimensional creators!

We rise together from this perspective in raising the collective consciousness of the universe and of Mother Earth.

Our dreams are wonderful ways to test out what we desire or want in our life, for example. You can go to bed at night and decide to work through a scenario of your choice to determine if it would be best for your highest good or not. If it works well for you in your dream then you can choose to apply it in your daily life in a conscious way. Enjoy the fun as a creator!

Perhaps the most difficult aspect with the sixth chakra is the willingness to surrender to the invisible, benevolent energies of the universe and to simply trust the process and know that even when some things do not occur as you would have expected them to, that when it is the right time, all will be well and an even better outcome will await you that you could not previously have foreseen or imagined. For this reason it is fundamental that you can trust your intuition as this does not come from your logical, practical mind.

When the sixth chakra is out of balance the reason may be due to:-

- a deficiency;
- an excess in that chakra or

- a combination of both a deficiency reason and an excess reason.

Given that the sixth chakra is all about vision it will not be a surprise to know that poor physical vision is a deficient characteristic. Poor memory and a lack of imagination are also attributes of a deficient sixth chakra. An expansion of these characteristics extends to someone who has a problem with remembering their dreams. A good way to improve this is to have a notepad and pen at the side of your bed so that when you awaken with a vague memory of a dream you can jot down right away what you do remember. The repetition of this exercise is an action to the universe that you are serious about wanting to remember your dreams and over time (different time period for every individual) you will find that your memory for dreams considerably improves. Cool!

After the passing of my beloved mother I can still remember an inability to imagine my future and having a wonderful life again. Every time I attempted to visualise what I wanted to do it was like hitting a brick wall and absolutely no ideas or creative stimuli whatsoever entered my mind. This was most unlike me because usually I am never short of creative ideas and innovative solutions to problems. It was a very challenging period for me and was as if all my energy and aliveness had been sucked out of me. This was, of course, part of the grieving and healing process through which I needed to flow in order to reset my own inner guidance system.

Past life regression can help greatly with restoring balance to the Ajna chakra and I found that doing this on a daily basis for about forty-five minutes left me feeling very free

and uplifted. It was as if the regression stripped away a hidden layer of 'stickiness' and dead weight to do with my present and past lives each time I did it. Indeed, I used to look forward to doing the regression because it made me feel so good.

With so much going on in the world at present it is very easy to receive mixed messages that do not always make sense and for misinformation to play their role in this. Such information may also desensitise us to what we would otherwise view as a compassionate situation. Remember that what you resist will persist until you can change the way you perceive something and understand that there is not only one right way to interpret an issue. The old, linear way of thinking has a person believing that there is only a right way and a wrong way to problem solve. Wake up! We are in a new energy paradigm now and you are a quantum being. When you can release all the old thoughts about how you have always seen and done things and can accept that there are new ways of thinking that can open you up to a vast new vista of using your intuition, then you will find yourself more in touch with your feelings and your ability to listen to your own inner voice of guidance. Always make a space… for intuition! This will help to rebalance you!

The more you live in balance and harmony the more your physical eyes will be restored to normal.

When we are truly accepting of seeing a situation in which we find ourselves, we are no longer in denial of what is going on and can figure out a beautiful outcome for ourselves when we tap into our inner power. There is a serenity and inner calm that comes from mastering the ability to see a situation or predicament for what it is and having an inner strength and 'knowingness' that we are always protected to proceed in our lives with what is for our highest good. The element of the sixth chakra is light. Does this ring a bell perhaps? My mother was also reminding me that no matter what situation in which I found myself there was always light at the end of the tunnel. Now I can understand and appreciate this phrase with new meaning, with enlightened meaning. We are beings of light. As we expand our inner wisdom and live in harmony we become filled with more light. Light is information. When we send light to a solution there is an innate feeling of positivity that a suitable outcome will present itself. It is beautiful and priceless to experience such trust in the universe. It will guide you through any situation and bring you great calm through the most challenging of times... if you allow it!

Every human being has this same power. It is for you to choose to tap into this inner space of awareness, intuition and creativity.

Examples of an excess sixth chakra relate to someone who experiences a difficulty in connecting with what is going on around them and feels unable to face what they can see. When we can learn to accept all facets of ourselves for who we are now and also learn to accept a situation head-on, safe in the knowledge that the universe always has our back and is continually protecting us, then we are able to make the changes that we need to make in our lives to restore our inner strength over our experiences without stressing or feeling overwhelmed. We gain clarity in our thinking that rebalances our physical body and our energy body.

In extreme cases, a person may suffer from hallucinations. Such an excessive sixth chakra characteristic may be brought under control when that individual can feel surrounded by beautiful white and golden light. The beauty of the light is its ability to help heal the imbalance and encourage the person to feel protected and guided in all they do. This healing exercise can be applied to any situation and is not only for such severe cases of discomfort and disconnection to one's body and spiritual development. It can also be an excellent practice for children who are suffering from nightmares. As the 'Old Souls' are reincarnating at this special time to help guide others throughout the Shift, any who experience nightmares may welcome a suggestion of white light that triggers a memory from a past life that, 'Of course it can help! They had just momentarily forgotten their magnificence and inner powers'. It may provide much comfort and peace for them.

When we can learn to let go of all negativity and let light into our lives, a beautiful flow to life happens and there is no longer a fear of the unknown because there is the inner confidence that life always brings us what is best for us.

If you enjoy meditation this can be wonderful for helping to dissipate stress and reconnect with the essence of your beautiful soul. We are each learning our own way to reconnect with the divine creative source, God, spirit that will enable us to consciously live a life of serenity, fun, abundance and love. If meditation does not appeal to you then perhaps art therapy and colouring books may be more interesting to you to help improve your imaginative skills and help with colour visualisations. A combination of these activities could be to sit in silence and imagine yourself going through each of your chakras from one to seven and back down again using the colour visualisation associated with each chakra. This can be a very powerful and transforming way to shift energy in your body for a positive outcome. It is another way of getting the physical energy moving throughout your body so that you do not harbour 'energy blocks' that are no longer serving you. Moreover, for as much as you are sitting relatively motionless for this colour meditation, you may be surprised at how fresh you feel afterwards. This is due to the old energy clearing out of your system. When you purge old energy out of your body it creates space for integrating new higher vibrational energy that transforms and empowers you.

Your inner wisdom whispers to you through the power of your intuition. If you are extremely unhappy with your life then only you are able to create the new person that you want to be. It starts with an awareness of what you want to change and an enthusiasm to develop your inner self with love, care and tenderness. When you can look at yourself as you are today and accept yourself for who you are today, you are on the road to a bright future that is of your creation.

So what else can be done to heal and restore balance to this sixth chakra?

Suggested Affirmations to support balance in the sixth chakra are:

I am able to remember and manifest my dreams.

I have clarity to see life in all its dimensions.

I am open to the inner richness of the truth within me.

I am very intuitive and listen to my first intuitive thought.

I have a vivid imagination that can transcend all dualities.

I release all established programs and patterns and meld with my Higher Self.

I can see the pattern of negative repetition and know what to do to correct this.

I no longer live in the image of illusion and live my true self every day in joy.

I surround every challenging situation with an imagined circle of light that helps guide me to the best solution for my highest good and the highest good of all involved.

When you can tune in to your own love frequency and listen to your own heart-beat, imagine how connected you will feel to everything and everyone around you. Let your body connect to who you are. All of your senses will be heightened and some of you may even find you have a particularly stronger sense of colours and heightened sense of smell and taste. It is all good! Listening in love restores a sense of wholeness of who we are and what our purpose is on planet earth. Know that every choice you make affects your vibration. Choose high vibration and coherence of your heart!

What is stopping you from having perfect health?

Whatever it is for you, we all have times when the fog drifts into our minds and we seem unable to see clearly. You have the opportunity to discover for yourself how to revisit a scenario and find a solution to your desires. All of a sudden the fog will lift and you will be blessed to enjoy your goal of perfect health or something else.

The ability to transcend the dullness of duality
Requires commitment and a desire for practicality
We are being asked to consider what it is we value
In order to be self-reliant, self-sustained,
authentic and true!
~ Lady Wise

CHAPTER 9

Chakra 7
A Crowning Opportunity

The most precious gold is peace in your heart
The jewel in one's crown chakra journey
This reward is for you when you live moment to moment
And trust completely in your energy component!
~ Lady Wise

Energy in our human body is our most precious resource. Consciousness is energy. This has already been scientifically proven. What is consciousness? It is a word that we hear about but which often seems elusive regarding its meaning. I know that I have frequently questioned and challenged what it is and have come to accept that it is so much bigger than my own thought process because consciousness has no boundaries of existence. It is quantum. It is multi-dimensional. It is our unit of thought which is infinite. It affects our wholeness within and out with the body. It is needed for us to think, to speak, to do and all the rest too! Where we are

at presently in our evolution of consciousness is so early in its development that everyone is learning and growing about what is means as well! Sometimes it is not necessary for us to always know the meaning of something because that in itself diminishes its sacredness. I feel sufficiently happy merely stating that our every thought comes from it and it is connected to us and evolves with us at a singular level and simultaneously at a collective human level, because we are connected to all that exists.

When a person heightens their level of consciousness to a very high state of thinking then they experience a bliss and a wholeness that takes that person out of their body momentarily and they experience the 'oneness' of the universe. This will be a different experience for each person and is very personal to them. When it does happen it is a very special and privileged moment which has been activated by other time lines too and comes together as a result of the energetics of who that person is. Having experienced this myself I found it totally liberating and joy-filled. I felt constantly joyful for at least three consecutive weeks after my experience and to this day find it difficult to express the words of such a sacred and personal transformative event in my life.

Every human being has the right to know that they are magnificent and a part of the creator source. It is your birthright to have the right to truth, the right to knowledge and the right to accurate and complete information. This is the right of the seventh chakra. The development and balance of this chakra focuses on our ability to think for ourselves and question those aspects about which we want to know more and/or to seek validation. In the seventh chakra stage learning plays a key role. An individual with a healthy and

balanced crown chakra will naturally seek knowledge throughout their life. As my mother used to say to me frequently, "What is it (life/existence) all about?" Bless her! She always admired my ability to believe in the unseen realms with such commitment and conviction. Yet, she affirmatively believed in God and would remind me that God always answered her prayers. Can you appreciate that there is no right or wrong way to connect with the creator source, God, spirit, Higher Self or that which is by another name? Without realising it she was probably just as connected if not more than me at that time. There is no competition, there is no comparison needed, there is no judgement, there is no prejudice for we are each stellar in our evolution in our own way!

The new human will create things that we do not have today through higher thinking. It concentrates on 'new consciousness thought' and how we create new things. Kryon has already been able to give us the projections of the inventions that are based on the consciousness development of what is now seen.

Your physical body allows you to experience the wholeness and 'oneness' of your sacred vehicle. The major lesson in feeling love starts with self-love. It has to, because how can you give love when you have not yet known the beauty and wonder of receiving love yourself? Love is the ultimate healer of all dis-ease!

With higher consciousness comes higher thought, higher intuition and inventions start to occur. All basic problems such as water purity and its present lack of abundance will be solved. These solutions are coming. Kryon explains that these are all true, all accurate and all with precedent, even today.

The human being and our related biology, however, are the most profound and dynamic in their connection. This is a revelation that will have many human beings asking for their seventh chakra program to be upgraded. As a human being becomes enlightened there is the understanding that we are connected to our own cellular structure. Presently, most people think of chemistry and medicine as things that are done to the body without the person being able to take any responsibility for the health of their body. With enlightenment comes the 'Aha moment' that the human being is the Commander of their cellular structure too which includes the 8 metre wide invisible field that is around them and which holds not only 90% of their DNA (still termed by many professional medics and doctors as 'junk DNA' because they do not understand it) but which also holds that person's Akashic records from all their previous lifetimes on earth and all future lifetimes on earth. Is this now too weird for you? Remember that you are a multi-dimensional human being. There is no time and space in this quantum dimension. This in turn means that you are able to tap into a future lifetime of yours and pull in the solution to a problem that you need in this lifetime.

For now, let's focus on the main ability to tap into past lifetimes for solutions to today's issues, remembering too that this ability to tap into to past lifetimes is equally not linear and so there is no time and space with this either. It simply is. Kryon describes enlightenment as:-

"

An evolution of consciousness into the realisation of who you are.

Do you understand the beauty and the power of knowing that you have full creative control over you and your whole body? With this knowledge and 'enlightened understanding' this means that you can with free choice choose always to have good health. A cold, the flu, cancer and Covid-19 would never become a health issue for you, because all disease (or dis-ease) with the knowledge of who you are cannot touch you. In your higher thinking state you are living and loving life in a higher energy.

Disease is a low energy attribute. Low energy cannot get to high energy. When all of your chakras are aligned and in balance you are 'at ease' with knowing who you are. There is no 'dis-ease' consideration as part of your thinking of any kind. It is not in your world of reality! This is fairly new information. Slowly, one by one, as human beings resonate with the core truth of this information not only will they become happier, more loving and kinder souls but they will live longer and be dis-ease free.

With the accumulation of this higher thinking across the planet over time (and of course due to the free choice of the human being it cannot be determined specifically when this will be) there will be a marked reduction in those human beings who contract any kind of disease. Can you imagine the extent to which this good health enjoyed by so many from this higher thinking enables not only healthy bodies but is the foundation for expansion of new inventions to solve current day issues? Light is energy. Light is information. Human beings feeling so healthy will have created more light within themselves which is infectious in a positive way and will encourage others to openly ask what they are doing to look so good and love life so much? This is what you can do. This is the power of who you are. This is when you will be able to tell them your story of how you became a higher thinker of love and compassion too!

Most of the human beings who are feeling the core truth of this information first are the 'Old Souls' (named this on account of the hundred or more lifetimes previously lived on this planet and not defined by linear age). They come to know that they can change their own reality by how they think.

Can you begin to comprehend how significant the recent outbreak of the coronavirus pandemic (Covid-19) is in relation to:-

- The interpretation of 'coronavirus';

- The chakra to which this 'speaks';

- The meaning and importance of this chakra;

- How you are thinking at this time?

Another word for corona is 'crown'. In the Chinese language, 'virus' is also translated to mean 'opportunity'. This is no coincidence! At this moment in history we have a unique 'crowning opportunity' to take time to realise conceptually and spiritually more about who we are. The invitation to you is to find a quiet space and to simply sit and be loved by the creator source, God, spirit, the source of all that is, where you can start to receive information for you personally in a multi-dimensional way in love that is core truth. This is the fast-track way to connecting with your Higher Self.

This first wave of coronavirus is going to give rise to the first major split of humanity on this planet. There will be those who start to shift in their thinking and begin to rise

above the dysfunctionality of living in a linear way compared to those who will continue to live in linearity in fear. The two key energies which are dominating Mother Earth at this time, in this age, are love and fear. As I have previously mentioned, love and fear cannot co-exist.

The seventh chakra is the 'Crown Chakra' governing the top of the head cerebral cortex and its Sanscrit name is Sahasrara meaning thousand fold. It is often depicted as the lotus flower with the thousand fold petals. In older times, the meaning of the thousand fold was another way of expressing the infinite. The basic issue concerns the cognising or innate 'knowingness' of realising how the feminine divine and the masculine divine within each of us come into equilibrium, thereby enabling that individual to find the 'oneness' or wholeness of their whole being with the divine consciousness of all that is.

This entanglement becomes more than just a connection of spirit with matter, consciousness with corporeal physicality and the unity of the feminine divine with the masculine divine. It is the beautiful manifestation of a human being who has come to know the two-way communication that is available now (to all who seek it) through the power of love in their heart. This heart coherence combines with the pineal gland and the brain as the computer, which opens up an individual to their inner wisdom of the universe. Furthermore, it opens up that person to unlimited potential in all they create with peace and love in their heart as an eternal given for the highest good of the universe, the human self and others.

As previously mentioned in Chapter 7 concerning the heart chakra, my abbreviated term for this is "The Triad is CIA"

– the combination of the heart, the pineal gland and the brain all working together in love and balance will result in Compassion In Action. This is the new human. This is what becoming enlightened means. It is when the human being realises that there is so much more to them than their corporeal body, their ego (which centres on themselves to the exclusion of holding a genuine caring for others with love and kindness) and limited possibilities of the mind's own intellectual thinking. That human being will instead focus their intention and daily living from a place of higher thinking that cares for humanity and is the beginning of an evolution of consciousness when collectively human beings mature and realise that their wisdom comes from the universal creative source of love.

A person does not need to be intellectual to find their way to wholeness through love. Love is the way! The heart coherence already experienced by many 'awakened' human beings around the world is when the human becomes aware of the importance of the heart and the pineal working with the brain to connect to spirit. The physical body or vehicle is your sacred temple which is used to manifest your dreams, desires and creations. The heart chakra is at the centre of the seven chakras. When your seventh chakra is balanced with your self knowledge and inner knowingness, then you allow the two-way connection with spirit through your heart on this journey of self discovery of your own essence and truth of who you are. It is beautiful! This is mastery. It can only be achieved by the human self but then this opens you up as a potential guide for others based on your story. Let us inspire one another on this sacred journey as we each light up and spread our light, love, laughter and compassion on this evolving Mother Earth!

What does this have to do with the coronavirus (the 'rona')?

Firstly, remember that all disease is a low energy consciousness. This 'crown virus' is a wake up call to humanity to kick-start those who choose to ask, "Is there something more to my life than my corporeal existence?" As soon as this question is asked to the universe in integrity and sincerity, change will happen for the highest good of that person that will elevate them to a higher level of consciousness than the average level of the mass population at that time.

Also please remember at this point that low energy cannot get to high energy. Therefore, when a human being is making time for themselves to question more about their own existence, in doing so, that person is starting to raise their own level of consciousness, even though they may not realise this. Just by commencing this action sends a signal to the universe that they are choosing a different reality in which to live (a reality of higher consciousness) which is naturally then taking them out of the low level consciousness reality that is followed by the rest of humanity who are not yet in control of their own existence. This one question asked by the individual is effectively giving the universe permission to step in and support the human being in a loving, benevolent way. The road less travelled to consciousness, to self-knowledge and to wisdom is for all who choose it without exception. There are no rules, dogma, doctrines, group meetings, event locations, time-tables, belief systems or religious scriptures. There is only love.

Have you noticed that acts of kindness, love and compassion have accelerated greatly since the pandemic was announced by the WHO (Worldwide Health Organisation) earlier in 2020? As crisis after crisis is unveiled across the globe, more and more people are becoming increasingly compassionate. They are consciously choosing to, metaphorically speaking, 'push their ego back into its box' and instead, think about how they can help others. These individuals are able to coherently link with the world around them and resonate their responses from a state of balance. They listen and respond to the information that is communicated to them from a position of understanding the knowledge that is imparted and discerning what is truth, all from the calmness and peacefulness of their loving heart.

What is the power of love? What is the impact of love?

At any time, but especially at this time of the pandemic, love and fear cannot co-exist. Over recent months, so many people have felt afraid on hearing about the pandemic and this has triggered worry, anxiety and a huge wave of fear that preceded any physical viral infections. This reality of low energy consciousness also brought with it unprecedented change in lifestyles and dramatically harboured restrictions on daily life which exacerbated mental health issues among some humans. Every day seemed like ground-hog day, filled with uncertainty, more fear, economic problems, accumulating financial worries, company bankruptcies, media overreaction and endless discussion including potential chemical vaccination cures that, when first discussed, were at least eighteen months away. In other words, a very frightening environment in which to live demanding 'self-isolation' without a person able to feel in control of their life, no time-scale for getting back to normal and indeed, often constant media talk that no normal would ever exist again. The perfect storm of doom and gloom.

An example of the corollary of the previously mentioned devastating daily scenario would be the following:-

The melodic sound of a black-bird singing from a neighbour's cherry tree gently wafts through my open window and I rise to a new day of hope, joy, love and abundance at approximately 5.20am. After a long stretch I sip a glass of room temperature alkaline water enriched with minerals and go outside to do an hour's gardening before the sun rises. The elementals listened carefully to my request put to them the previous evening, to ease the weeds for me to pull out thus minimising the disruption to Gaia's animal and insect species. Using an expensive pair of secateurs, these robust beauties are perfect for trimming down wandering branches that have escaped from the architectured impressions of my garden reality. With my basket full of nature's surpluses, I almost trip over the local stray feline whose call reminds me it is time for a breakfast smoothie and a gifting of a little milk for her. After twice filling my trug with weeds and garden debris I surrender to an amazing smoothie concoction of spirulina, banana, turmeric and water. Minutes later the sun shines brightly into my kitchen reminding me of the dawn of a new day and new beginnings in my life. As always, I salute to Mr. Sun with the following respectful rendition (sometimes the spoken word and sometimes sung):-

Here is the sun, awaken
From the oceans, the oceans deep
Climbing the heavens, heavens highest in the east
Here is the sun awaken!
Here is the sun, awaken
From the oceans, the oceans deep
Climbing the heavens, heavens highest in the east
Here is the sun awaken! Here is the sun, awaken
From the oceans, the oceans deep

*Climbing the heavens, heavens highest in the east
Here is the sun awaken!*

A brush of my teeth, lippy on, spray of fragrant perfume and a quick change into jeans, t-shirt and my current favourite whale-watch Iceland jacket (currently named as such because I purchased it specifically for my intended Iceland trip which was disrupted by the lock-down restrictions and so I missed the whale-watch...for a second time, the first time having been in Cape Cod when my friend and I slept in and literally missed the boat! Ha!) readied me for a local walk in nature before most people would even be awake. For me, this is the best time of the day. On the way out of the door I throw a mix of sunflower seeds and multigrain bread pieces on to the back yard for the birds, then I head out via various fields passing only a few houses and farms. It is usual to greet a couple of ducks calmly resting in a local burn, comment to the daffodils on how beautiful and graceful they are looking, pass by five softly snoring Tamworth pigs and speak to a few sheep, lambs, crows, the occasional thrush, horses, foxes, geese, cows and chaffinches along the way. The air seems so fresh and I stride out grateful for such a privileged time and location in which to nourish my sensate realm.

On returning home I usually rush to thoroughly wash my hands, change out of my walking shoes and whale-watch Iceland jacket before cooking up some porridge with fresh kiwi fruit, a tea spoonful of much loved Manuka honey topped with a handful each of sunflower and chia seeds. Mmmmm, delish! All of this gratefully lived and it is not even 9am yet! As I wait patiently for my porridge to cool down a little bit I contemplate what today's excitement will be. One of the great privileges of this lock-down period is that there are few date and time stamped tasks that must be done. It creates a HUGE space for allowing one's creative mind to step forward. Allow me to share a few examples with you as follows:-

1. *Selecting a large paintbrush and bucket from the garage, filling these with warm water and then painting this across the old wallpaper to weaken the adhesive before stripping off the walls;*

2. *Playing with several inexpensive jars of plaster filler together with a general purpose scraper, which has been used as both a scraper and trowel for smoothing the plaster to fill holes;*

3. *Finding an old tin of white matt paint and using the cleaned large paintbrush from item 1 to freshen up skirtings and doorframes;*

4. *Seeking out old pottery planters and filling these with small stones in the base to act as a water filter, topping up with multi-compost and planting seeds from daffodils to plan for more flowers next year;*

5. *Purchase of ingredients and grease-proof paper in preparation for baking a fruit cake to enjoy with morning coffee or afternoon tea;*

6. *Vacuum cleaning the sitting room and shifting around furniture and paintings to create a warmer feeling to my home (which is in the midst of a renovation);*

7. *Sitting down in my dining room with a few notes poised to allow the poetic juices to flow with a poem to celebrate the Diamond Wedding of a friend's parents.*

Local stores have become my new best friends for feeding my creativity and meeting both food essential and creative essential needs under lock-down! It makes my visits such fun as I explore the possibilities of utilising 'tools' which I have never used or even considered before. How exciting! I am learning new ways of doing things and keeping myself occupied for very low cost with great personal satisfaction and joy! What is there not to love? At 11.11am I tune into the universe and send love and the violet flame around the world to transmute all negativity into more positive energy. In the afternoon after making up a mixed salad for lunch I usually sit down and write. As the sun sets a little meditation keeps me balanced for the day and I send reiki round the world to go where it is needed. Before long it is time for preparing dinner. The time has passed so quickly. A little telephone and text connection catch up with friends and it is time for gratitude to the universe before sleep. All good!

The two days are poles apart just like the polarity of a human being. The difference between both days would be down to the mindset, health and balance of each individual and the extent to which one individual was living their joy each day with heart coherence in excellent health, thinking loving thoughts while the other person was still living in survival mode uneasy with their situation, afraid of virtually everything in their life, unaware of the power of their ability to realise a different way of doing things for themselves that would empower them and set them free from a life that was fear-based in a low energy consciousness where disease was prevalent and their likelihood of contracting every cold, flu and ailment that was going around was very probable as a result.

There is not only one reality for more than seven billion people living on the planet. Do you understand this? You have the power to create your own reality with the awareness, wisdom and understanding that is attained, when the seventh chakra is fully open and spinning in harmony with all the other chakras in alignment with your physical body and your spiritual essence or soul. Essentially, you are opening yourself up to the expansiveness and unlimited universal field of collective consciousness, which is the oneness of all that is. This life force that permeates your being gives you your aliveness, your radiance and your vitality. It also gives you your eternalness!

"

Liberation cannot be achieved except by the perception
of the identity of the individual spirit with the
universal spirit.
~ Shankara

Look for the change in your eyes! When a person has flawless sparkling eyes, for example, it is an indication that they are full of vitality and in good health. They will naturally attract other people to them with their enthusiasm for life generally and because they have developed an inner peace that enables them to control their emotions and deal with all circumstances and situations including any conflicts that may arise. You can have the 'love power' of sparkling, vital eyes and good health and become a person in whom others trust.

"

Be confident in your emotional expression and use
your voice to empower others and guide them in lesson.
~ Lady Wise

Your confidence will grow to the extent that you will find a solution to every problem that comes your way…if you want it.

With kindness, a greater expansion of your intuitive abilities through loving yourself more and accepting the creative powers within you, will build your self-confidence and your happiness will grow. As you grow in confidence you will hold a strong sense of self-worth and because this allows you to recognise and be accepting of the deep connection within yourself, you will be able to relate well to the people around you.

A calm countenance will manifest from the inner wisdom that you remember and your belief that you are responsible for your own happiness governed by what you think of yourself. This awareness and responsibility for your own actions develops your self-confidence and you then give permission to yourself to flow with the experiences of life in infinite love.

As an eternal optimist who believes that everything works out better than I could have imagined it, I will thrive in a reality that is very different to the world in which a pessimist exists. As a person who allows love in my life starting with loving my own body as it is, I will attract a higher vibration than someone who does not love their body, looks at it as if it is independent from them and seemingly drags it around with them everywhere they go. As a person in my daily life I operate a new habit pattern of responding rather than an old habit pattern of reacting to everything. This is the way of it.

Everything originates from an idea. The concept of this idea commences its journey in the crown chakra. As creators, therefore, we are effectively sourcing all our ideas from the great central source of creative existence through our own spark of divinity which is linked to the cosmic consciousness filled with universal divinity.

At its purest, my understanding therefore is that no idea is ever truly our own because we are connected to creator source and there is no separation. Each of us, however, is so unique in our talents, gifts and skills that it is the extent to which we are then able to manifest this conceptual idea into our reality which gives it our own personal touch. This is quite an evolved thought, far removed from those egotistical third chakra thoughts of separation and self-identity that would have the human self claiming all ideas as their own.

An individual still entrenched in their life with the ego dominant, will not realise that in every nano-second when a person has an idea, so too have probably at least two other people on the planet! Hence the reason Charles Darwin with his book titled 'On the Origin of Species', literally pipped Alfred Russel Wallace to the post with the submission of his own theory of evolution by natural selection. Apparently, Alfred received relatively scarce notoriety for his excellent contribution and yet he had been working on it up to twenty years earlier.

The fact that an idea may be picked up by someone else too emphasises the importance of action without postponement. A delay in manifesting your ideas may mean that others manifest something similar within a shorter space of time if they have a better and more disciplined ability to manifest, and then you will be disappointed that you did not act sooner.

Change is happening. Love is a multi-dimensional energy about which we are just beginning to understand with our mind. Our heart is the centre of our 'being' here on planet earth. It is at the centre of our light body, our Merkaba. When our chakras are balanced and we are 'tuned in' to the Field, to the consciousness all around us, we flow naturally with these beautiful energies in life and find solutions to the issues that cross our path with ease and grace. There is no struggle. There is no fear. There is no judgement. There is only love. This is how we evolve with all these changes.

Allow your intuition to guide you as it supports you in a gentle way. Remember that when we resist changes, they persist until we wake up and listen to the lesson for us. These lessons are different for each person because each person is so unique and magnificent on this planet. At the core of this love is the love for our self and our cells. Your body responds to you moment by moment even when you are not consciously aware of this. Every thought counts! Every thought affects your body and your cellular structure. This organism that is your vehicle while here on earth in this lifetime is always responding to you.

Every feeling is sensed by you and your cells. How are you feeling today? Is it possible for you to see your body as an intelligent body? What can you allow to change within yourself today? As you embrace change, how you see your beautiful vehicle will start to influence your thoughts in a different way. It will slowly begin to alter the old program inside you. Your higher thoughts will open you up to your higher consciousness and to enhanced creativity. It is your soul's desire to allow yourself this gift of the new you, the expanded being that you are.

At any moment, you have the free choice to ASK the creator source, God, spirit, Higher Self or another name to which you address it for support in expanding your consciousness. Remember free choice is sacred and absolute. You will have to ask because it is in the nature of asking that you give permission for the beneficient, loving energies to work with you in supporting your desires. Otherwise, they will not intervene out of respect. There is the understanding that you do not want any assistance.

These invisible energies of light only ever have our best interests as the focus of their attention. You are so dearly loved. They are all around you, 24/7, even while you sleep and they hug you and hold you in a quantum way, in a unified field of consciousness and love. Can you feel into this? This is the feeling of connection. You are creating this for yourself. If you are unsure of your next steps or an idea that you have, then ask for validation (but do not expect a linear answer because spirit only works in a quantum way). Spirit does not work in a linear way. Spirit cannot work in a linear way because this dimension is constrained and limiting. As a human being we are beginning to choose to learn a reality which is not linear taught. We are awakening to the fact that we are multi-dimensional beings even although we cannot see these other dimensions yet. As Kryon explains we are lifting ourselves out of linearity. It is for you to take responsibility for your own life. Feel what is right and appropriate for you. Remember each one of us is so unique that we each require different information at any one time. I especially love Alkazar's definition of responsibility as 'the ability to respond in the moment'. It is not about reacting, but responding...even when all you can think of doing is to smile!

Recently Nick Harvey's father, Paul, at eighty years young, created a beautiful musical composition from four random notes that Nick gave to him as part of an improvisation game that the two of them used to play. Although Paul Harvey has dementia, his 'magical improvisation' went viral and the BBC Philarmonic recorded the piece. Moreover, Nick noticed how much more mindfully 'present' his father became in his company in those weeks since he had been playing his music. This is simply one example of the qualities of the quantum human being. When, as a human being, we are fully engaged in our multi-dimensionality and in the present moment, we are effectively outside of the linear matrix that limits most of us in our everyday living. Music and art are the two best known creative outlets to bring our quantumness alive at this time.

In a new energy, we are evolving to learn quantumly, absorbing information from the quantum Field. There is no time-table to this evolution. Recognise the beautiful divinity inside of you, because this is the eternal part that is love. Take your time!

"

The Field is a multi-dimensional soup of potentials that already exists for civilisation, humanity and every single human being.
~ Kryon

This quantum thinking is by definition not linear. Linear learning is an old energy patterning. Now it is time for positive change. Don't worry! There is no requirement to become enlightened as soon as you have finished reading this book! Ha!

We each have the most beautiful entourage of energies working behind the scenes to guide us and to physically manifest our

co-creations. It is up to each of us to believe that we are always in the right place at the right time to move forward with our dreams with ease and grace. Every detail experienced in your life is for you to acknowledge. The expansion within you is all about being a creator. It is your birthright to live your potential! There are no limitations to your ability to create in love! Trust in yourself, trust in your heart and trust in your soul that you are taken care of and all is well.

The magic is in your openness and your desire to move forward and flow smoothly. Your vibration will start to magnetise to you the next step that is for your highest good. You will be able to create and in this creation you will attract abundance to you on all levels (including health, career, relationships, money). This is not something that is done for you. You create this from within as a result of your own love and vibrational frequency.

You are here on earth to be the difference! You are responsible for your own evolution and can ask for energetic support at any time but especially when you are feeling a little low. Simply find a quiet space and just ask spirit in a relaxed manner what you need to do to move forward in a particular situation with ease and grace.

Similarly, when you are flowing with life and feeling so happy, this time is a wonderful time to share your joy with the energies and invite them in from your open heart to say, 'Thank you, bring me more!'

The energy of appreciation raises your vibration and you are closer to your awareness of the seventh chakra. Science is already demonstrating this fact. Your intention and your desire to change yourself and to radiate more love is what changes your life experience. Your vibration will reflect back

to you what you are giving out. When you are appreciative of something, then the universe works with you to bring you more situations in which you will be ever more appreciative. It is simple! There is no complexity in this. Any complexity is manufactured by your mind. You are learning a new way of conscious communication with your soul. It takes courage to be you! I have every confidence in you! If I can do it, so can you...if you want to!

The reality in which most human beings presently exist is one of chance. Next time someone remarks to you that you are very lucky, feel free to respond that you are creating your own luck! You, together with consciousness, have control of chance. Perhaps you may also like to take a look at the Global Consciousness Project undertaken at Princeton University, USA which proves the science of this.

When we share ideas and creativity in love, compassion and unity with each other we are creating an even bigger difference through this collective activity rather than alone. The potentials for the increased power of love when more than two people come together and share an idea for the highest good of their neighbourhood, a community and beyond, is immeasurable. When this idea is manifested in love, its repercussions are felt by everyone at a deep level as it sends out ripples across the lines of time and becomes forever impactful on the galaxy. This world is expanding with your help, love and creativity. This is where your energy is coming into play. You are evolving as the new human as your contribution to the evolution of humanity. Your only task is to be the love that you are!

You have the free choice to take energy and consciousness anywhere you want it to. This is real. It is all about your belief. Do you believe it?

The belief is the key.
For the belief itself is generated by your choice
and the God inside.
~ Kryon

You are not in the world by chance. Everything can change for you right now when you believe in love. Remember love is multi-dimensional, it is not linear. The creative source of the universe knows who you are. The only thing you need is your awareness!

There is hope for the planet and you are it! When we think differently we heal our 'sacred' selves and we heal the land with the thinking that we are one with all that is. We are all Gods and Goddesses on Mother Earth, expansive, limitless eternal beings of light touched with this divine spark of creative source to create, create, create in a unified field of energy that is always supportive, benevolent and loving. We are becoming the new humans on earth as we experience these Changeover Years (2013-2027). With awareness, knowingness and inspiration we can do it together in this playground of life and truly feel the connectedness of the collective consciousness (this positive impactful dynamic force) with which we can align that lifts us out of duality and into a reality where dreams are manifested and we can thrive.

Sadly, there are still so many people with dreams who struggle to lift themselves out of the low level consciousness of survival and decide to give up on these passions because they never question that there is something more to life than their physical body that could ever elevate them to grander more graceful experiences and potentials! I hope that you will be inspired to become a new human and know the difference.

When I first started attending yoga classes taught by Yogi Nirmalendu there was a reception room in which we would all wait. On top of the table in the centre of the room was a variety of books and every time I was drawn to the same esoteric book. I would avidly read a few pages before we were ushered into the next room for our yoga class intently focused on every word and keen to absorb its essence and meaning. It's all these little things on my own soul journey that I am able to 'witness' at will which make me chuckle and very grateful for each experience as they all contribute to my wholeness.

So what can be done to heal and restore balance to this seventh chakra?

Suggested Affirmations to support balance in the seventh chakra are:

I am a magnificent human being guided by my own inner wisdom.

I am one with my divine spark of spirit that resides in me and is eternal.

I always keep an open heart and an open mind to new ideas.

I came into this world with strength, power and a support system of divine energies who guide me for my highest good.

I know that my soul's energy is travelling with me and ask for guidance on the next steps of my path of light.

I ask to receive the call forward of gifts to work with my cosmic energy and give permission for this work to be done.

I am learning to grow in wisdom and in love every day.

I open myself to freedom, my inner guidance and the joy-filled limitless dance of the spiral of life.

The sign of a healthy seventh chakra of understanding and knowingness with the universal field of consciousness (which is energy) reveals itself to us when we feel fully alive and vital in our 'beingness' every day. We are able to tackle both day-to-day issues and longer term issues with a calmness, ease and grace that bring solutions, often new solutions to what we need to thrive. Continually we have a sense of the bigger picture and live with a loving connection in our heart that reassures us that there is unlimited abundance in all things – relationships, career, friendships, money as examples. The concepts and ideas created in the seventh chakra are given meaning and vision in the sixth chakra as we descend down through the other chakras to the first chakra of manifestation. The illumination of being part of something bigger than ourselves brings with it a maturity of higher thinking and wisdom. When this is applied to the fifth chakra of communication we are inspired to follow through with our ideas and concepts in a compassionate way. The fourth chakra lovingly allows us to be considerate in our solutions and our will of the third chakra drives forward our desires to be transformed with feeling and exuberance into manifestation. These new programs within our physical vehicle no longer associate with the ego of 'me, mine, more' which dominate those human beings who choose to remain in a reality of duality. Remember that the ego never disappears from the human being. When a person expands their consciousness, it merely allows them to control the ego and to 'put it back in its box' while they take care of what is needed.

I am an advocate for teaching progressive 'new era' psychology based on our most highly conscious people so that we understand their strengths and some of the unlimited potential of what such magnificent human beings are capable. This would be open to everyone who wanted to know.

Each person carries within them a divine spark that is eternal, non-judgemental and magnificent which is connected to all that is and which is like a golden thread that connects us to our eternal home, the creative source, God, spirit or by another name. It is in every one of us. Most of the population at this time have still to make a choice point to go within themselves and find the God or Goddess within.

Perhaps you would be kind enough to let me know how it feels to be a God or Goddess?

Chapter 10

Feeling the Joy!

"

Good health and wealth are inextricably linked
To our state of balance and how expanded we think
All dis-ease is imbalance in our body's kingdom
It is time to awaken, heal trauma and claim our wisdom!
~ Lady Wise

Did you know that the old English for wealth means 'well-being'? Indeed, the origin of 'weal' is the word 'wel'. This denotes a state of happiness or good fortune. A good life is available to every soul who chooses to take a leap of faith and lead with their heart. The most profound awakening is happening across the world for hundreds of thousands of individuals. We are identifying with who we are at a very deep soul level and much healing is occurring at the same time. One way to heal trauma is to meditate. Allow me to explain different ways of meditation that may surprise you! There is more talk about meditation than ever before and yet I regularly encounter individuals who are unsure what it is and who are keen to know more. Not only that, but

there are many other people who have the perception that meditation is a complicated, complex spiritual practice. For those who choose meditation with such complexity and devotional act, there is no judgement. It is my passion to explain in this chapter the simplicity of meditation for all to enjoy its healing qualities. I would like your meditation to be a little reminder of the light that you are and quality connection time for you to feel healed and restored to good health and radiance with all pain, worry and anxiety dissolved.

In the Eastern world, meditation has become an important daily activity for millions of people. In the Western world, however, many of us have been slower to take up this practice simply because of cultural differences that perhaps have not placed sufficient emphasis on the benefits of this activity. A lack of understanding and/or no practical information will always inhibit the popularity of such an exercise. Thankfully, the wonder of using the internet has brought meditation to a wider audience and stimulated curiosity among many more. All good!

Allow me to communicate the joy of meditation from my own experience and to reinforce at the outset that it does not require any special equipment, clothing, other type of gadgetry or even demand a particular location for an individual to do meditation. It is one of the most normal things that a person can do for themselves on a daily basis to help them to balance. This is frequently why individuals choose to create an opportunity for ten or fifteen minutes early in the morning to undertake meditation before the 'busyness' of their day. In this way, the benefits from doing a meditation can provide valuable nourishment for your body so that you can address your tasks in a relaxed frame of mind with clarity of focus, creativity and vitality for enjoying the day ahead.

The benevolent love that is all around you in the universe waits patiently for you to be open and accepting to receiving this unconditional love. It waits for you to feel this energy flowing through you in such a loving and peaceful way.

Did you know that walking is a meditation for some people? This can simply be a walk in your local area when you consciously choose to be aware of the smells, different textures around you, even listening to the sound that your own footsteps make with every step. This rhythmic pacing from your own feet can be very soothing to a person. Each step carries with it an individual beat of 'life force' energy. If you are fortunate to be close to a park, fields, nature trails, hills, lakes, streams, rivers or able to rest in your own garden, then you may delight in listening to nature's symphony of bird song, for example, as meditative inspiration too.

Alternatively you may be more interested in meditation that requires no thought and no other movement from you. When you become too focused on your mind then you can miss out on divine inspiration from intuitive messages. All you require to do is to completely relax. Allow, allow, allow and trust that this beautiful energy that is available 24/7 will be received by you and refresh your chakra centres in harmony and love.

When you receive this creative source energy, it is so energising because it is pure love. There is no judgement of you. This is unconditional. I would encourage you to welcome this fresh, new feeling of rejuvenation throughout every cell of your body without the need for the minutiae of how it all works.

Most individuals do not understand the linear and multi-dimensional quotient in relation to what was, what is and what will be! Humanity is evolving with a multi-dimensional perspective after having always lived in a linear way without being aware of the consciousness of multi-dimensional thinking. This is very challenging because we are not built to understand this. What has this got to do with meditation? When you are able to totally relax, be still and simply allow yourself to be loved, then you feel the love surging through your body. Love is not linear. Love is multi-dimensional yet most of us do not question what this is. Do not decide anything about what is going to happen. This is how it is done. This is the difference between multi-dimensional thinking and linear thinking.

The love of Mother Earth, Gaia, Pachamama will feel so good. When you choose to open this metaphoric door to understand more about yourself you are giving permission to connect with your beautiful heart centre chakra and all that is. The strength of this connection will fill you up with love in a way that is indescribable because it is so unique to each person. This explosion of overwhelming compassion will make you realise that everybody has a soul. All new things that you may need to know will start to be imbued into your consciousness. You will be amazed at the positivity of how your life may be changed.

You do not have to be intellectual to be loved. You do not have to understand every little detail to be loved. You have the potential for mastery and all you need to do is sit down, take a deep breath and be loved by the amazing invisible energies which are all around you that wait for you to give permission to feel the love. You are loved and known by God, Creator Source, Spirit, whatever name you choose to give it.

When you go into a meditation it is your unique opportunity to get to know yourself better. No-one else can take you into this sacred space. You must be open to finding this extension of yourself within. It is beautiful! I am love, you are love, we are love. This love is within you. This love is who you are and it waits to connect with you and uplift you. Whenever you have a question about your own being, then question this and wait for the validation of this to come to you. There is much to discover about yourself beyond the physical corporeal body that you see when you look in a mirror!

In this period of The Shift discussed in Chapter 1, it is as if every human is programmed to awaken to the joy of who they truly are as a whole human being at different times. It takes free choice for the human being to ask if there is something more and then time for us to become acquainted with our multi-dimensional side and the fact that the soul is multi-faceted.

"

Confront your fears of rejection
And with feeling, navigate your intuition
We are creating Heaven on Earth
This is the gift we've been given since birth.
~ Lady Wise

One of the ways to counter stress and to reconnect with our heart and soul is to exercise the breath. When we do this pausing and deep breathing it provides a space to receive the intuitive messages to come through.

Exercise

Find a comfortable position where you will be undisturbed for at least fifteen minutes, preferably half an hour.

Inhale deeply, hold the breath and exhale that breath very slowly.

Imagine when you are inhaling, that you are breathing in only positive energy to take you forward in your life with joy, happiness and abundance.

When you are exhaling your breath, imagine all the toxins and deep, low energy that has been holding you back for so long, being released from your sacred body.

Inhale deeply and exhale that breath very slowly;

Inhale deeply and exhale that breath very slowly;

When you breathe in deeply and slowly

Release all tensions in your beautiful body

Allow yourself to completely relax.

Sometimes it is helpful to focus both the in breath and exhaled breath to a specific part of the body. You could start with the soles of the feet and work up through your body using the breath inhalation and exhalation in turn with each part such as the knees, abdominals and lower back, stomach, heart centre, throat, arms and shoulders, face and top of your head.

Allow yourself to be in a place of receiving the invisible waves of love that are there for YOU!

Afterwards, surprise yourself with how rejuvenated and refreshed you will feel!

New beginnings!

*In Duality there is always the beauty of contrasting dark
and light
With our own free choice, we have power with clear sight
Grounded deep in our enhanced intuition,
We can grow in love and wisdom with inner vision
It is the energies within ourselves that constitute our power,
All we have to do is to feel balanced and claim our
mastery in every waking hour
We are allied to nature, can you feel her soft kiss?
As she leads you with gratitude to your own world of
bliss
Know that you are blessed to align with the 'oneness' with
grace in your heart
For we're at the change of an era that's offering you a
fresh start!
~ Lady Wise*

CHAPTER 11

Dancing with Good Health!

"

The gift of the breath touches all of our being
The beginning of new thought starts with feeling,
not seeing
A smile on your face and peace in your heart
Will have you dancing with good health from this
rebirthed start
We are sitting in a time of no prediction,
Trust in yourself with unerring conviction.
~ Lady Wise

The thread throughout this book has been that joy chases away disease and restores in you a peaceful countenance and well-being that intuits continued good health and happiness for as along as you are in your physical body. The key is balance, and from this balance the moment to moment peaceful existence that now exists within your heart, relaxes your mind and body totally. This comes from your ability to see something from a higher perspective. There is an understanding of what you have come to know and of what you have changed permanently. This realignment between your physical body and the call of your soul has brought with it a greater maturity in you and a greater awareness of what it is that you want from your life going forward. You trust in the universe, in its 'wholeness' and listen to your inner voice that 'all is well' always. Balance broadcasts balance! This is the power of metaphysics!

*When you have one balanced individual in a group
of those who are not or amongst chaos, people begin to
feel the one that is balanced and their balance
then creates other balance.
Many times this happens without conversation.
It is simply one attribute among many that is
starting to occur on this planet.*

~ Kryon

Light begets light! Light actually creates more light in a way that is difficult to explain. Light is not confined to boundaries. It goes everywhere. Just think of a huge stadium filled with thousands of people all sitting in darkness. When only one person lights a match everyone else in the whole stadium can see it, if they choose to look at it. This is the power of light. This is the power of you, for you hold a divine spark of light, of consciousness within you. We all do, it's just that most of us don't yet know it!

As Kryon says, 'When we can see one another then we are not afraid of one another!' In certain ways, we are all the same. The stadium (that is the whole earth) becomes filled with light. The internet is allowing us to see and recognise this with greater clarity. It has allowed and is allowing so many people to realise that those of different cultures are going about everyday life loving one another. You see it is not so different around the world! We have such an opportunity to awaken to the grandness in understanding one another with compassion and a desire for caring.

In this way, slowly we can begin to understand that when we look into the hearts of those that we have not seen before that we are all equal and we are all one. Once again, let me remind you, everyone matters!

Both aspects of our divine feminine essence and our divine masculine essence, regardless of our gender, exist in every human being. Only when we are able to acknowledge both these sides exist equally in ourselves (representing duality), can we then become whole and express ourselves through this wholeness as a balanced, harmonious and joyful human being.

The divine feminine essence encourages us to embrace truth, harmony and compassion in balance with assertion and drive to achieve our dreams for the highest good of ourselves, but also with a transcended understanding of the wider universal impact. The missing aspects of the divine feminine have resulted in an overpowering of masculine essence primarily expressed in a low vibration of aggression, corruption, fear, bullying, power grabbing and selfishness. The time for such low vibrational thinking and actions has to go. Universally and globally, we are ripe for higher vibrations of love, compassion, peace and harmony to be at the forefront of a change and a new world.

Living on rumours, gossip, and drama leads to negative consequences, a deflated light in our beautiful vessel of energy and lower energy in an individual. Every positive thought, word and act enhances our light within and is restorative

for our DNA cellular structure. Those who choose to live a life broadcasting gratitude, forgiveness, joy and love will find themselves with more energy to live their life. This is how the divine intelligence is starting to work with humanity.

How are you choosing to show up each day? Are you hopeful, full of gratitude and feeling energetic at the unknown surprises and adventures that the universe has in store for you or do you still feel lethargic, afraid of venturing out into a new street, space or shop because you are still clinging to old belief systems that are no longer serving you? Either way there is no judgement. We live our lives with choices and the choices that we make. Always remember that you never really make a poor choice. It will always serve as a lesson for you on your soul journey. I am merely suggesting that with a subtle shift in your mental and emotional well-being that you can awaken to an awareness deep inside you that has love and joy at its core to sustain you through the toughest of challenging situations. It is all about embracing a new way of feeling and a new way of experiencing the power of your own energy. We are learning to become 'spiritually mature'.

Moreover, we are moving beyond a world of conflict, war and destabilisation, one person at a time, with every individual who awakens to their essence of divine love within.

"

What is the fast-track to enlightenment?
The ability to sit down and be loved.
~ Kryon

Always know in your heart, YOU DO NOT NEED TO BE SMART OR INTELLIGENT TO BE LOVED!

Many people have built an imaginary shield around them, but in the new energy since 21 December 2012 there is no longer a need for this. When you can drop your shield and forget everything that you have been taught, in that moment you will be neutral and let the love in. Then you understand how to react to energy!

You do not need to build a shield around yourself – you are shielding EVERYTHING – INCLUDING BALANCE!

There is no need to worry about anything. How many of you are making things up so you can worry because it has become a habit for you?

When you can sit and be loved it can rewrite your program of what is to be for your life. You are a unique and magnificent human being and sadly, certainly in the Western world presently, the teaching of this core truth is not yet the way of it. Much work has still to be done!

The Essence of You!

Stop waiting for a better now, for this is the right time and the right place

For you to awaken to the joy of living life with ease and grace!

Treasure the oneness within your being resonating with creator source

Trusting that everything happens for you for the highest good of your inner light force

A person who is weighed before they die and weighed again after their death will weigh exactly the same

For the soul that resides within your body is infinite and unable to be contained

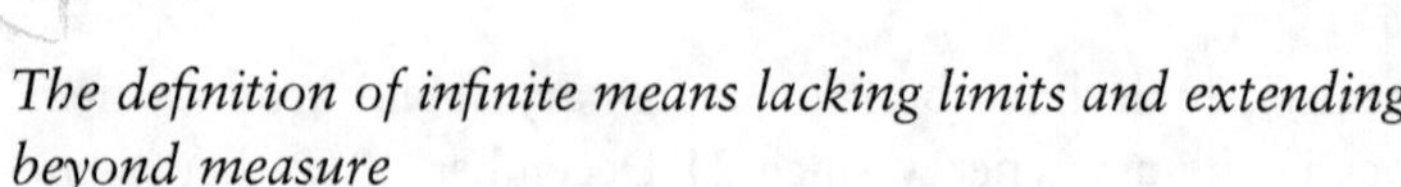

The definition of infinite means lacking limits and extending beyond measure

This is the joy of who you really are as you live as spirit in your temporary physical vehicle of pleasure

Your divine spark within is connected to all of creation

It is for you to self discover its existence and master the skill of manifestation

If a person restricts who they are to the corporeal world of physicality

They will never rise above this illusion of reality called duality

Confined to status, reputation and material wealth accumulated

Such dominance by the ego drives humans to become discombobulated

For there is no separation of the rest of the world from you

So please just take a moment to suspend all the things you believe to be true

You have the key to the universe within you waiting patiently to be unlocked

This divine intelligence is always with you, it is only your thoughts which keep it blocked

Perhaps consider a shift in thinking that changes the concept of yourself

Which suppresses the strength of your ego and opens you up to your Higher Self

It's up to you to give yourself permission to follow your bliss

For when you do the universe will miraculously support you in this

The essence of you, though invisible, merely wants to forever create and expand

You are dearly loved by the universe; will you allow it to take your hand?

When you attain balance and are in a coherent oneness with the creative source

A long-lasting human who is resilient to disease will be the outcome, of course!

~ Lady Wise

This is the gold of enlightenment. God is love. The creative source is everywhere, which means it must be in you too, because there are no exceptions. I am God. You are God. We are God.

The Masters who walked the planet wanted us to emulate them, not worship them! They would do miraculous things and talk about love. Their energy was of such high consciousness from living a life of pure love that this allowed them to be able to manipulate physics with their minds! One of my friends, Anu, witnessed this with one of the great Masters named Sai Baba. He was personally invited to a private viewing hosted by Sai Baba who manifested for Anu a beautiful gold ring complete with a precious stone feature. In fact, my understanding is that Sai Baba would manifest all kinds of beauty in the form of gifts for the people who came to visit him on a daily basis.

Today, the energy of this planet is shifting. You can integrate the love and compassion of the Masters and give people love and compassion. This is infectious as well as being healing. Dis-ease can leave the body of those next to you because you are balanced. This is what is infectious about light.

Have you noticed the power of laughter? Laughter can create laughter. This is light! This is the beautiful part of compassion and joy! It is not in a box. It escapes so quickly and is so infectious that it usually catches people unawares! Many of my friends and associates have commented over the years that if ever I become lost when I am out with them then I should simply laugh and they will recognise it and come running to find me. They tell me that my own laugh is very infectious and very funny to listen to. I often amuse myself and burst out laughing. When there are other people around me who share the fun and then start laughing too, I regularly then expand my laughter because I start laughing at the people who are laughing with me. It is such a great tonic without the gin, albeit my sides are usually aching afterwards and my mascara runs with the tears of joy that stream down my face. These moments are always so spontaneous, so hilariously funny and unrepeatable. What is wonderful, however, is that such laughter is a mood changer and it doesn't take long before the most serious person in the room displays at the very least a mild, wry smile. All good! When you are living in your joy and in balance you will spread the light to others. Balance is the key!

Thankfully, today it is not seen as unusual to say, 'I believe in metaphysics'. Showing love, appreciation, gratitude and compassion is attractive to all. Most people are keen to hear more about what I have to say and what I do. Light is attractive and compassion becomes even more attractive! This is how others will respond to you too when you live a love-filled, joyful life too. Your enthusiasm for life is infectious. The Greek root of this word comes from 'enthios' which means 'The God' and 'iasm' which means 'within'.

The test of our brief existence here on planet earth is to discover with free choice the difference between thinking that we are separate from everything else and that our physical self is all that exists with a focus on what we do, what we have, how much stuff we can accumulate and being concerned about what other people think about us versus the awareness and 'knowingness' of the existence of our Higher Self, spirit, Creator Source, God or whatever you would call it by another name, which is the divine particle that is within us which wakes us up when we decide to follow our passion, come what may.

When we follow our bliss and do exactly what we want to do without anyone telling us how or when we can do it, then life becomes effortless and the universe starts to support us in ways that are indefinable. They are unable to be defined because they are not linear and/or logical. The magic of love will start flowing into and through your life, working with you to enable you to do whatever it is that excites you. This is the essence of you when you are doing this! This is spirit at play! It is your responsibility to go your own way! Remember that there are many pathways for you to explore. When you learn to navigate your life from your heart centre, with an inner confidence that whatever the universe has planned for you will be in your best interests and show up at the right time for you, it feels like an adrenalin rush through your body that imbues you with fresh energy and a zest for life. With this ability to respond to whatever life has in store for you, your true life path will be supported and give you comfort and serenity around not necessarily knowing how this will all come together.

The wind is at your back. You have got help.
Now go do it!
~ Kryon

When you awaken to the universal consciousness and realise that we are all connected, your desire to follow your passion becomes self-evident. Moreover, you realise that your passion will not only serve you, first and foremost, but will naturally attract to you others who will benefit greatly from your creative choice.

For example, if you choose to become a singer or an artist then it will surprise you how others who share your passion will seek out your songs and art respectively. It is so easy now to have a global platform from which to promote yourself and your craft. When we are in the flow of our being we are increasingly experiencing our wholeness. This will become attractive to others who will probably ask you why you are so joyful. New possibilities for co-creating on new projects and collaborative work will emerge from the unlikeliest of sources. How exciting!

One of my mentors over the past twenty years with whom I had the honour of meeting back in 2012 was Dr. Wayne W. Dyer. Throughout writing this book I dipped into some

audio of this meeting and was reminded of his very wise words that he wrote down while he was in the Navy and only 19 years old.

Don't die with your music still inside you!
~ Dr. Wayne W. Dyer

Whatever is aligned with the creator source, spirit, God is who you are. It is the essence of YOU!

There is nobody who is in any way different from you.
Once you understand yourself you have understood the
whole humanity.
~ Osho

It is for each of us to choose to be curious and to find out if there is indeed something more than the linear, logical life that most of us live. I hope I have inspired you to open your heart to the richness and abundance of the universe that is there for you, for in this quest of self-discovery you will find your own resonance and rhythm of life which is uniquely priceless, yet which can create for you a very peaceful existence with longevity of life and all the joy, good health and wealth that you could ever want.

Personal, complete and total peace will create a
very long-lasting human who is resilient to disease.
That is the secret to long life.
That is the secret to health.
And that is being peaceful to the point where you are

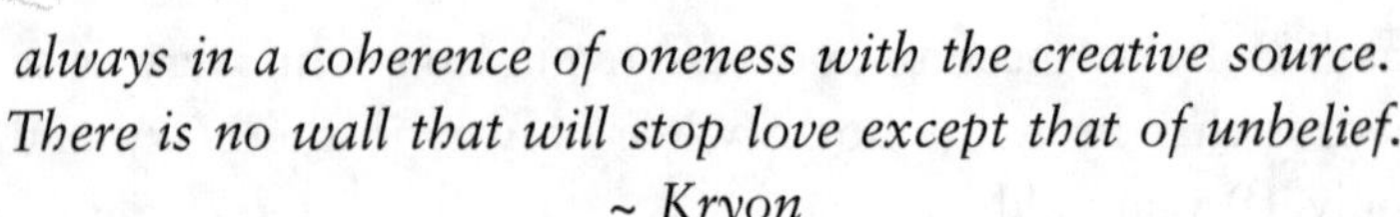

My mother was full of wonderful phrases and quotes and aware of my fondness of horses. She would often say to me in her soft, gentle voice, "You can lead a horse to water but you cannot make it drink!"

There is no-one else who can help us unless we consciously help ourselves. This is the lesson in the spiritual growth and maturity of humanity. As we mature in our quantumness, we become less drawn into the linear model of past, present and future and realise that it is this moment now that is the real living, the real reality.

Children are wonderful at teaching us the power of living in the NOW! Animals are even better at teaching us this joyous life lesson. It is all about finding our happiness in this moment, finding our joy in this moment, feeling alive in this moment. This is truly living a great life and dancing a joyous dance. There is no conundrum. It is simple. The whole of existence is connected, including you and can support you, but cannot do it for you.

It is through your own free will that you will choose your next step. You will never be judged by the creative source for the direction in which you go, because you are a piece of the creator source and not apart from it. There is only a united overwhelming universal love for you in all you do.

Blessed and Free

Never before have I felt so blessed
So free in my heart filled with happiness
The game of life waits for you to explore
Will you choose to participate or this gift to ignore?
Know that you are enough and never alone
Wherever you travel may your heart feel 'at home'
There is no separation of your existence on earth
We are all one with Gaia and have been since birth
Rejoice in your aliveness of living the dance
In excellent health you've created, without chance
Enjoy the adventure of transforming your passion
Remembering the currency of compassion is in fashion!
~ Lady Wise

Conclusion

Only Love Matters

In everything you do it's time to consider the art
Of balancing technology with the love in your heart
Pure love is a core truth that we can understand
As part of an evolution of humanity using the tools at hand
Love and fear cannot co-exist
So stop allowing the fear to persist
You are here to love and accept the wholeness of who you are
As a human being of brilliance and a shining star
Awakening to this awareness will transform your energy
Enabling you to break free from debilitating lethargy
Give yourself permission to experience that loving feeling
As you give intention to what it is that you are needing
Step by step adapt to circumstances with ease and grace
Trusting that spirit has your back and you are ALWAYS in the right place
Learn to relax into every experience that comes along
Expect things to go right for you and never to go wrong

Wake up each morning and welcome in another love-filled day

As you resist the need to panic and can cast all doubts away

For when you choose to hold a higher thought of gratitude

It shifts your entire energy body to one of positivity and aptitude

You are gifted an opportunity to appreciate

All things that love can facilitate

Feel the freedom to prioritise what matters to you now

And allow your innate and consciousness to deliver to you the 'How?'

We are remembering that we are allied to nature and Mother Earth

As we listen to the call of the soul embodying healing and rebirth.

~ Lady Wise

Nature is a multi-sourced phenomenon. When you are not connected to nature you do not feel the circle of time and experience the non-linearity of life.

It was Lao Tzu who said,

"

Nature does not hurry, yet everything is accomplished.

As multi-dimensional human beings we have forgotten the importance of our quantum connection to all that is. Without our connection to the 'oneness' of the universe, we are unable to tap into the unlimited abundance and potential of all that is. In a linear world of individual separation, a human being has limited potential because they remain disconnected to the divine spark within themselves. They allow their ego to dominate their thoughts and life decisions. Many are even proud of their linearity and in their naïvity consider that they have conquered life itself. This is the power that the ego has when it is not brought under control by its owner. The consequence is that the person continues to live their life under an illusion and never 'wakes up' to the freedom of the liberating energies that are available to support them in a transformed, compassionate, loving way.

Free choice is absolute. It is very important not to judge yourself...ever. We are all experiencing an 'awakening' at different times and in completely unique ways.

Remember that in a victim world, life happens to you, but in a loving world, life happens for you. Who are you really? Your good health depends on the choice points you make. There is no judgement, just don't make a mistake! Ha! Ha!

"

When there is love, laughter, good health and celebration
in the air
There is no space left for us to contemplate
A life of negativity, depression and suicide
Only the joy of the moment in which we preside!
~ Lady Wise

A new energy is here. It is the difference between a linear world of black & white or an amazing multi-dimensional reality of colour, excitement, opportunity, invention and good things coming. As a manifestor of a new reality, you are starting to work in colour. Indeed, you may know from your own experiences in life to date, not everyone can see this metaphoric 'vision of colour'. Kryon expresses this beautifully stating, 'You cannot explain colour to a sightless person' but those ' Old Souls' who are aware, are being drawn to one another around the globe to co-create and collaborate on new innovations and new solutions. May this message change your thinking for your highest good and allow you to see a little more colour!

Sending you blessings of continued joy, abundance and good health!

"

The game of life waits for you to change your reality
Create healing for yourself, good health and vitality
You are here on purpose, with freewill to experience
Your aliveness as part of and trust in the universe!
~ Lady Wise

About The Author

Lady Wise is a heart-centred entrepreneur, life and business strategist, Reiki Master, Chartered Accountant, singer/songwriter, inspirational speaker, poet and author who is passionate about improving the healing and living experience of individuals. It is her dream for every individual to feel that they are fulfilling their potential in life once they choose to recognise, accept and reunite with the divine essence, that divine spark of spirit, which is part of them, resides within and which is also part of all that is in creation. She inspires and assists human beings on their journey of self-discovery and personal transformation to understand their own life purpose, thereby enabling others to enjoy a self-fulfilled life in a multi-dimensional world of adventure, joy, love and good health. She believes that success is by far the most fulfilling and rewarding fun when you are doing what you love and are co-creating and collaborating with others.

One of her many dreams is to manifest a Centre of Excellence for Healing and Consciousness that would ultimately become the blueprint for other centres around the world. There are many doctors of medicine who are great healers and Lady Wise is enthusiastic to participate in the design and build of a magnificent practical structure for them to be able to work together with a selection of other healers and energy workers to greatly improve the healing experience for so many. It would be a collaboration of skill from the higher thinking of individuals who know and understand that consciousness is physics. It is the science of physics that allows for spontaneous remission to successfully occur in adults and for homeopathy to work. In this progressive building, they would be able to freely practise 'Q5 Healing' which addresses the human anatomy and energy systems giving equal prominence to each of the following aspects:-

- A person's soul consciousness;

- A person's energetic field health;

- A person's mental health;

- A person's emotional health and

- A person's level of physical health.

She already has some draft sketches in mind of how it might look and is expecting to attract the abundance in all its forms to make it happen in divine time!

If you have enjoyed reading this book and would like to expand your compassionate, business and esoteric knowledge then Lady Wise would be delighted for you to take a look at the Other Books of Interest section to choose your next exciting read!

Other Books of Interest

Compassionate Care Books

FEEL THE LOVE: 111 TIPS VOLUME 1
WHEN VISITING SOMEONE IN HOSPITAL

Want to solve an immediate problem for your friend or loved one who is in hospital and are unsure how to help?

Are you unconsciously increasing the anxiety of your loved-one in hospital?

Would you like to reduce the stress of visiting a vulnerable relative in hospital?

111 tips are broken down into eleven chapters to help reduce stress for both in-patients and visitors, as witnessed through the eyes of a 'carer' with no medical qualifications but a passion for improving your healing experience.

A catalogue record for this book is available from the British Library.

Paperback: ISBN: 978-0-9933513-2-7
EBook: ISBN: 978-0-9933513-0-3

FEEL THE LOVE: 111 TIPS VOLUME 2 WHEN CARING FOR SOMEONE AT HOME

Want to solve an immediate problem for your friend or loved one who is still living at home and are unsure how to help?

111 tips are broken down into eleven chapters to help reduce stress for both you and your loved one, as witnessed through the eyes of an unpaid 'carer' with no medical qualifications but a passion for improving the healing and living experience at home.

A catalogue record for this book is available from the British Library.

Paperback: ISBN: 978-0-9933513-3-4
EBook: ISBN: 978-0-9933513-1-0

Lady Wise is keen to extend the 'FEEL THE LOVE' series of books as a source of inspiration to those individuals seeking more hope, love and compassion in their daily lives.

Esoteric Books

LOVE IS THE WAY!

Do you act on your gut feeling too? Earlier on 19 May 2018 I had viewed the Royal Wedding of Their Royal Highnesses the Duke and Duchess of Sussex and was so inspired by listening to The Most Reverend Michael Curry's sermon on the power of love that I had the idea to create this book. I hope to encourage you to connect with the love that is inside of you to become a happier, balanced and calmer person living in harmony and love wherever you are and doing whatever you choose to do. I appreciate that each of us must 'self-motivate' to be empowered. We must each create with total clarity of mind what it is that we want coupled with a sense of deserving, love and graciousness.

We have allowed ourselves over the generations to close off our emotions as human beings and thereby deprive ourselves of the greatest joy on planet earth that one can imagine – the joy of feeling, expressing and giving love!

This is a non-religious book that invites you to enjoy, embrace the truth and be exuberant in creating your own success, abundance and happiness through the joy of 'love power' and expect the unexpected!

A catalogue record for this book is available from the British Library.

Paperback: ISBN: 978-0-9933513-4-1
EBook: ISBN: 978-0-9933513-5-8

Esoteric Books

KNOW WHO YOU ARE!

* Due For Release 2021 *

For more than twenty years I have been especially curious about life, my life, and who I truly am in an esoteric, metaphysical way. This has led to several epiphanies of laughter, joy, love and self-discovery! I am passionate about imparting my knowledge when appropriate to others and allowing the free choice of every human being to further question and know who they are.

When my uncle in Australia fell seriously ill in 2016, I felt a compelling need to write to him and impart what I had learned about the puzzle of life. I intuitively believe that every single lifetime builds a library of wisdom and I wanted to share this esoteric knowledge with him, 'old soul' to 'old soul' before his physical departure from planet Earth.

I started to write to him most mornings and evenings and have modified the letters slightly for ease of delivery into 111 letters for you to read. These letters are of a personal story unfolding between two 'old souls'. I hope this book will be a source of inspiration to those individuals seeking their own truth of existence, enabling them to better understand their reason for being.

With greater insight into our spiritual existence, each one of us can stand in our truth and enhance our intuition using our sacred heart. The beauty of life itself can be yours!

Poetry Book

POETRY FROM A PLEIADIAN

This 3 in 1 poetry book
Invites you to take a look!
It contains a selection of
111 poems
Divided across three sections:-

Foodie Fun
Miscellany Mixture
Esoteric Truths

Laugh your way to a higher vibration
with this upbeat collection of playful
and insightful verse.

There is nothing more delightful
than laughter and love!

Lady Wise is a heart-centred entrepreneur
and an influential Wayshower
in these Changeover Years.

A catalogue record for this book is available from the British Library.

Paperback: ISBN: 978-0-9933513-6-5
EBook: ISBN: 978-0-9933513-7-2

Set Of E-Books –

FINANCE AND BUSINESS STRATEGY
BLENDED FINANCE (SERIES OF 6 BOOKS)

This series of business & financial books targets Business Owners and Managers, Entrepreneurs and Directors who have been in business for at least two years, who are keen to accelerate business performance and continue to grow a sustainable company in the new era of compassion!

Volume 1 *"Look After Your Assets!"* gives you greater insight into the potential risks specific to the account balance of fixed assets to which your business may be exposed and what action would be appropriate to anticipate, mitigate and act on risk promptly.

Volume 2 *"How to Manage Your Cash"* explains some of the risk areas associated with the account balance of cash in the balance sheet and sets out examples of controls to minimise these risks. In addition, Lady Wise addresses how to better understand the cash that you have in your business on a daily basis and imparts her knowledge about the importance of cash flow forecasting and how to develop your forecasting skills to determine cash inflows and outflows as a tool for improved future business performance.

Volume 3 *"How Well Do You Know Your Trade Debtors?"* will help you to improve your understanding of the sales cycle and explain how to focus on trade debtors and avoid any potential over-statement of this important debtor account balance in the balance sheet.

Volume 4 *"What Are Your Liabilities?"* explains the importance of evaluating what are your liabilities in your business to provide you with as complete and accurate records as is possible giving you control and knowledge over the account balance of trade creditors or accounts payable to which they are often referred. This guidance will allow you to understand your creditors and know where your money is going in the business to meet various costs incurred.

Volume 5 *"Are You Taking Stock?"* focuses on the account balance of Stock in your business and includes learning about the general potential error types that can arise in managing stock and how to minimise the risk of them in your own business.

Volume 6 *"M POWER!"* evolved from the creation, narration and production of a collection of 45 video vignettes by Lady Wise.

Claim your Mastery and self-emPOWER!

This book addresses key business success factors that will improve your leadership skills as a foundation for accelerated business performance and sustainable business growth in the new era. Sounds like many other business books perhaps? What makes this so special?

What is especially intriguing is that in order to achieve the desired accelerated business performance, Lady Wise explains that the foundation for this joy and success has its grounding and roots immersed and melded first in the personal transformation of oneself!